LEADING FROM THE ICE

KEVIN HARTZELL

Front Cover Photo courtesy of The Sioux Falls Stampede
Back Cover Photos courtesy of: Quinnipiac Athletics, The Herb Brooks Family and Stanley S. Hubbard

Cover Design and Interior format by The Killion Group
http://thekilliongroupinc.com

ACKNOWLEDGEMENTS

To Kim Cristofoli, thank you for all your unselfish help and advice throughout every phase of this book. You above everyone else helped me get through this project. I could not have completed this book without you. THANK YOU.

Tom Murray, thank you for your time and friendship and for coming up with the name of this book.

Jonesie and Z, you guys have inspired me often, thank you.

Lauren Baratz-Logsted, thank you for the great editing job.

To all the great coaches, mentors, friends and students in my life, some of whom are mentioned in this book, you are the treasures that have made my life the wonderful journey it continues to be.

Marybeth, your love and support is the reason I get out of bed every day.

DICK,

THANK YOU FOR THE GREAT SUPPORT OVER THE YEARS. YOURS IN HELPING THIS WORLD BE A LITTLE BETTER PLACE FOR OUR YOUNG PEOPLE.

Kevin

TABLE OF CONTENTS

INTRODUCTION

Once upon a time, one little ole junior hockey team in the state of South Dakota became the nation's largest feeder of captains and leaders for Division I College Hockey Teams in all of America. How could it be that South Dakota, a state more famous for herds of Bison and Mt. Rushmore, would out produce hockey-crazed states like Michigan, Minnesota and Massachusetts, would be the place where the nurturing and producing of so many major college hockey captains would occur? South Dakota? Not only were they producing captains-leaders throughout the college hockey landscape, but they were producing them for the very best college hockey programs in America, like Harvard, and Minnesota, and Michigan State and Notre Dame and North Dakota and a whole bunch more. Was it by luck or was it by good or even great design? What can we learn from this model in Sioux Falls? Can other sports or other industries replicate it and, in the end, do we even need leaders?

This book answers these questions through a study of real-life leadership. As a championship-winning hockey coach, I focus on my life journeys in leadership—what I learned from mentors at many levels of sport and industry and how I applied it to a group of young men and aspiring hockey players in my time coaching in Sioux Falls, South Dakota. This book is a reminder to us all of why leadership is an important concept in a free society and a reminder that we as a free society need to place more focus on the fundamentals of leadership in our society that is increasingly being influenced by other factors.

One team in Sioux Falls had an unprecedented record of success in the world of ice hockey with the nurturing of current and future leadership. Many leaders and mentors paved the path along the way—real-life people in real-life leadership roles, influenced others along the way. If the coach is right and we get better at teaching and nurturing leadership and teamwork, just maybe we'll have more successful young people leading ever more successful young people. Industry will grow stronger and more moral. Marriages will be stronger and last longer. We might even elect leaders and not politicians and in the end have a stronger country! You think? If we help our next generation realize their leadership potential, just maybe we can change the world for the better, one leader at a time.

PART ONE: HUMBLE BEGINNINGS

CHAPTER 1: IT TAKES ONE
TO KNOW ONE

When I retired from coaching the first time, I did not envision the possibility of being back in a "big game" environment like this one tonight. Getting out of full-time coaching, leaving the hockey profession and becoming an outsider just does not lend itself to this possibility. Yet as fate would have it, I am back in the game and this night may be one of my favorite nights ever of my professional life. I am coaching an outstanding Sioux Falls Stampede team and on a night where we need to win a game-four to force a deciding game five for the league championship.

As I stand outside our locker room, fans stream past me with trays of adult beverages to go along with their various arena food choices. I get polite greetings from many of the fans who compliment me and our team for what has been thus far a great final series. People here in Des Moines, Iowa are simply excited to be in "the house" on a night they hope to see the championship Clark Cup trophy presented to their home town team, the Des Moines Buccaneers.

I look about and love what I see. It's the Mad House on Hickman and it may be my favorite hockey arena of all time. This "house" gets its name from its location on Hickman Road, a busy east-west thorough-fare in the heart of Des Moine's west side. The arena is smallish by most standards, holding only 3500 seats. The blue and red wooden seats and benches are slightly elevated from ice level giving every one of the 3.500 spectators a great view from above the ice sheet. With the low ceiling, the sound and energy of the crowd reverberates making it seem like you are competing in front of 10,000 fans. It is a special place.

I cannot be more excited to start this game-four against a very good Des Moines team that will soon after the conclusion of this series have two first-round NHL draft picks in Kyle Okposo and Trever Lewis. Our Sioux Falls team has also has future NHL'ers in Zach Redmond, Nate Prosser, Ben Holmstrom, Cory Tropp and Andreas Nodl. There is a lot of talent getting ready in each respective locker room. I feel the excitement with every fan that walks past me.

My guys, my players are a steady stream in and out of the locker room, managing to wedge themselves through the Des Moines fans. This is not a normal site. Our training and equipment room is some 30 feet outside the locker room door. Our players have to go out of the crowded and primitive visitors' locker room and wade through the crowd to get to the training area. In there, await Kevin Ziegler, our strength and conditioning coach, and equipment manager Brent Johnson. Players get a final stretch from coach Ziegler or one of a variety of accessories from Brent. I remain amazed at how our players pass through the crowd of excited Des Moines fans almost as if nobody even notices them.

Knowing we have a coaching and training staff I am proud to be part of only increases my excitement level tonight. More importantly however, we are about to take the ice with one of the finest teams I have ever been involved with. We had won the regular season championship with a franchise record 43 wins. We were picked by most hockey observers to finish last! We accomplished this with a group of young men that many thought were "re-treads" of sorts. Many had disappointment with their previous teams in their previous year. Some had careers appearing to be dead-ending. They hadn't disappointed this year. They overachieved in every way.

We had won two tough play-off series to get to this series and this night. I am excited for our players and suspect they will play well. I have played a lot of hockey and many other sports as well, but this team…well it's a real team in the very best ways of a team. And when it comes to leadership, this group of young men all under the age of 20 could be roles models for much of society. This great collection of teammates and leaders representing the Sioux Falls Stampede will be ready for a severe test in an exciting venue. There is no doubt in my mind, that the leagues two best teams are about to take the ice.

When I came to Sioux Falls I wanted to focus on leadership as a core value of what we were going to mentor. In the months and even years leading into this night, it had been apparent to me there were way too many public displays of a lack of what our team had a lot of; leadership. No doubt each of us have witnessed through various news programs, and even up close and personal experiences, a lack of leadership in our society today. Society's failures include banking scandals on a world scale, corruption in government, poor marriages and even bullying on the playground. One could argue all of these failures in society happen at least in part due to a lack of leadership.

Often when I watch the various news programs, and listen to the various politicians they put out in front of us, I find myself asking: Where have the leaders gone? Why don't we see more leaders in our everyday politicians? Why don't we see more real leaders in our everyday lives?

Then I got to thinking and asking myself the question: *Where do we actually learn about leadership?* Some of us are lucky to have leadership role-modeled for us. Many of us are not so lucky. Universities, for the most part, don't offer courses and majors to teach leadership. I would think in a free society likes ours we would make leadership a valued ideal. So maybe in the end, the problem is us. We as a society have not placed enough emphasis on leadership, resulting in a real problem: we don't know what leadership is or even what it looks like when it is out there for us to see. Unfortunately, we don't even see it.

It takes one to know one is an old saying we used back in the day when we were kids. We used the saying often in jest, especially if one of our friends called us a name like a smelly skunk. Even at a very young age, we would return the "compliment" with a *it takes one to know one*.

Like many old sayings, there is a bottom-line truth embedded in it. To understand or recognize a value or trait in others, or ourselves, we often must possess or be familiar with the trait. As an example, like *it takes one to know one* implies, there is no one better at spotting a con man than another con-man. Con men know and recognize the tricks of the trade. The same goes for most skills and abilities. The same is true with leadership.

Once any of us are enlightened, shown the way of things, we will see it and recognize it readily. We have all experienced this when first shown a new car model, or a mannerism/habit in a friend is pointed out or any of a number of things. Once we recognize it we will see it without even trying. I know when my daughter bought a Honda Element, a square-shaped SUV, I seemed to see them everywhere I went. It wasn't that suddenly there were more of them on the road; it was just once I saw and recognized the vehicle, I recognized them without effort.

The same is true with a human quality like leadership. I am convinced we need to teach leadership skills in schools and nurture it in our various youth and adult activities. Our youth will benefit as will every relationship they touch and interact with. Once enlightened with what leadership looks like, our young people, our future leaders will see it and embrace it. Our society needs leadership in families, in industry and in government. A free society will not survive without it!

THE CLASSROOM OF LIFE

All of us are born with many gifts and talents. These gifts are most often shaped by teachers, mentors, friends and various life experiences. I have been as fortunate in this regard as anyone could hope to be. I believe I was born with many natural leadership abilities, but maybe more importantly, I have been influenced by some outstanding leaders and mentors. Subsequently, I have dedicated a good portion of my life to leading, teaching, and influencing others in the pursuit of excellence and the leadership required to realize success in any endeavor.

I grew up in St. Paul, Minnesota. Our family was somewhere in the middle to lower-middle class. I was the fourth of five children of Eugene and Delores Hartzell. Our dad was a life-long blue-collar worker. Our mom was mostly a stay-at-home mom, who when needing a little more challenge, took on jobs at the local hamburger place or one of a number of stores near home. My dad, was a member of Iron Workers Local #512. For a number of years, he served as the leader/president of that union. There were strikes and labor unrest where Dad's strong leadership abilities were put to test.

I was a playground rat, meaning I hung at the playground and played all day long. We played whatever sport was in season— summer, fall, winter and spring. We played baseball the most, but hockey was big too. I couldn't wait for the local ponds to freeze as they provided some of my greatest memories. In Minnesota, aspiring young hockey players' greatest asset was ponds that froze late fall or early winter. This happened most often before any substantial snow and before the playground ice was ready. The ponds were and still are today a Minnesota playground of their own. One of my dreams was always to own a home with a pond in the backyard so my kids would have this winter playground experience—a must in my eyes for a Minnesota family. This dream eventually came true.

My mom said I was an easy child to raise as she always knew where I was. I was most often at Sylvan playground just off of Rice Street and Maryland in St. Paul. Rice Street was known as a tough neighborhood, well known for both baseball and boxing as well as tough characters. I was the last of a generation of kids who went about mostly unattended by adult supervision, or at least not a whole lot of adult supervision. We hung out at the playground where we were free to play our own games, pick our own teams and learn where we fit in to a pecking order without an adult to explain it to us.

We were free to learn the ways of things from the older kids and having our hands in just about everything a kid could get his hands into. We flooded the ice rinks and dragged the infield of the baseball diamonds. We brought equipment out of the playground's *shanny* as we called the building, and picked it back up and put it away when we were done manicuring our fields and rinks.

The older kids taught us how to do just about everything. Eventually, we became the older kids, taking on the role of leader and role model and showing the younger ones the way of things. There still remains something quite romantic to me about growing up in that world, not overly intruded upon by adults. We learned lessons through the organization of our own play and every-day peer group interactions.

I am pretty sure many of these lessons are lost in today's world. Today's events are scheduled for our kids, most often with the directing and organizing of these events coming at kids from the adults. Kids often just show up and participate in whatever is thrown at them. It is hard to learn leadership skills when all the leading is done for you!

I was blessed with a little better-than-average intellectual ability. I became a pretty good student, not because I thought I was really that smart, but because I was competitive and willing to work. I wasn't going to fail or not do well in a class. I was too competitive to allow myself to fail in any way. At some level, I think I had some natural leadership traits and abilities, but leadership is still something I think has to be role modeled and learned.

I was lucky enough to find my way to Junior Hockey. After playing hockey at Washington High School, I made the St. Paul Vulcan Junior team in my hometown. It is here that I began to learn and recognize many of life's finer lessons about leadership and teamwork. I had a great teacher in our coach Doug Woog. For the first time in my life, I was involved with other young people who mostly had strong individual goals. This was a totally new experience for me on many levels and contributed mightily to shaping who I am today. I will come back to some of these experiences later.

In my opinion, I was always a better baseball player than hockey player, but I loved hockey. I mean I *loved* hockey. Hockey's not so big secret is that it is fun, more fun than any sport I ever played. Hockey practices are fun. Skating in itself can be fun. Hockey is also a challenge. In basketball, one or two players can pretty much bring the ball up court. Others can stand under or near the basket. In football, one guy throws it, others catch it, some block. In hockey, everyone has to be the quarterback at times, everyone has to catch it, and everyone has to defend. The sport requires a large number of skill sets. It is fast and physical and very competitive. How could one not love it!

During my Junior Hockey experience with the St. Paul Vulcans I earned a hockey scholarship to play Division I college hockey at the University of Minnesota. There I played for a time for legendary 1980 Olympic gold medal winning coach Herb Brooks. We won one national championship under Herbie and also finished second another year under his successor, Brad Buetow. I eventually became captain of that University of Minnesota team which I have always felt was an honor. I graduated with a BA in Psychology.

Like many others of my generation, we gained a pretty good education by taking on lots of different jobs as we grew up. Through my younger years I was a laborer for my good friend Joe Taney and his dad's home construction company. Joe Sr. made sure we did things right! I was a stock boy at JC Penny just out of high school, a steel mill laborer at North Star Steel as I was entering college (a job arranged for me by Herb Brooks with what I suspect included a message about a harder life). I was a golf course worker at the University of Minnesota Golf Course during my college years with lots of very early hours to be met.

All these experiences led to my employment as a hockey coach—my first major job after college. Since that first job, I have been a part owner and CEO in two different business ventures. Also in the past, I was in sales as a sales rep and eventually a National Sales Manager selling commercial airtime for a major market television station, KSTP-TV/ABC in Minneapolis. I have written a weekly hockey column for many years. In recent years I have returned to full-time coaching. In my desire to positively affect my fellow man, I have begun to run and help run leadership development camps, which are where I expect my future service to be.

I have been happily married for over 29 years now to the love of my life, Mary Elizabeth (Bidinger) of Morton, Minnesota. We have three wonderful children, Brandon, Eric and Whitney. We raised our family in White Bear Lake, Minnesota, with my dream of a pond in the back-yard coming true. All three of our kids grew up on ice skates, but our son Eric was the one who loved hockey the most. Eric would get up earlier than many other kids on a fall/winter weekend simply to go out and skate by himself. We are very proud of our three kids. They are all good people with good hearts. I feel like I have and continue to live the American Dream.

Through it all, it was my humble beginnings in Junior Hockey that awoke my senses to what great teammates and real leadership looked like. Though in my younger years I had seen leadership in people like my dad, my awareness and understanding of what leadership was had not yet taken hold in me. Each step along the way, with more knowledge and an ever-evolving understanding of what teamwork and true leadership looked like I was able to understand that many people because they don't understand, recognize or appreciate leadership, didn't see what was often-times obvious to me.

It does take one to know one! In my opinion, today's society is not seeing and recognizing real leadership often enough and collectively we need to change that. We need to nurture leaders and leadership as an important value if our great and free society is to survive, and this can be accomplished with a renewed focus on enlightening our young people on the fundamentals of leadership. Once they see it, they will always see it.

A GREAT LEADERSHIP LABORATORY—ICE HOCKEY

My practice of leadership development has had as its laboratory, the sport of ice hockey. I have been fortunate to have coached many years at the Junior Hockey level, which is basically a level of competition devoted to young people aged

16 to 19. I have been continually taught by these young people themselves; all a product of our collective society. They came from public schools and private schools and even from some of the nation's top prep schools. Some well prepared to venture out on their own, some not so well prepared.

The United States Hockey League, known as the USHL, is in my opinion the best amateur league in the world. The league attracts 16, to 19-year-old boys; many are the world's best amateur players, hoping to earn hockey scholarships to America's finest academic institutions. From the USHL many move on to professional hockey including the top professional league—the National Hockey League (NHL).

The USHL is kind of like a high school, a junior college and a trade school all rolled into one. Most of the USHL teams are located in the upper Midwest, from North Dakota through Iowa and extending a bit both east and west. The league thrives in towns not big enough for major-league sports, but big enough to support these USHL teams and their expensive operations. It is a bus league, meaning each weekend teams get on buses and travel to each other's hometowns to play one another. The travel is grueling at times but it is a small price to pay for young men who have high aspirations for their hockey future.

The opportunity to play in front of large audiences of fans who support their hometown team is special. More special, however, is the opportunity to play each weekend in front of scouts from the world's top professional league, (the National Hockey League) as well as scouts and recruiters representing the finest universities in America. The concentration of amateur talent in a single league has no equal anywhere else in the world. USHL alumni populate over 35% of all major college and university hockey rosters. Virtually every player on every USHL team will graduate to a major college hockey roster.

Each USHL player will have the great life experience of not only playing college hockey, but getting their education mostly paid for. The opportunities after college are equally appealing as NCAA Division I alumni populate over 35% of all NHL rosters. The USHL, American College, and the Pro paths are all tremendously appealing opportunities for young aspiring elite hockey players. Along the way, if the young man is so inclined, he will take advantage of a world-class education at one of America's great universities.

The path to higher-level hockey is not easy. Young men often leave home during their high school senior year, sometimes their junior year as well. They miss out on the traditional high school years that some say were the best years of their lives. They miss going to senior proms and homecoming games. They miss out on experiences with life long friends and high school sweethearts. They leave behind brothers and sisters at home, all to play hockey in the USHL.

The draw of the league is so popular that most young men don't think twice when asked to join a team. They get in their car with mom and dad in the fall of the year and drive to towns like Des Moines, Iowa, and Lincoln, Nebraska, to be dropped off, enrolled in a new high school, move in with a new family and do what they love to do—play hockey. And play hockey they do. For the first time in many of their lives, they will be challenged in ways they could only imagine. They will also be challenged in ways they never imagined. Individual competitors just as good, and often better than themselves, will challenge them. No more big-fish-in-a-small-pond syndrome. Many enter for the first time in their lives the *real* world of hockey.

Most young men are only partly ready for the challenge. Some of these young men have great parents who have been very involved in their lives. Some come from broken families and need adult leadership figures. Some have already refined social skills, but many do not. For many of these young men, their natural abilities have gotten them to this point of hockey elite stature. Yet many really do not know what it means to practice hard or pay attention to details or even what it means to be a great teammate. Many have been the focal point of their previous teams. Many have obtained borderline celebrity status in their local communities. But when they arrive in the USHL, they are just one of the guys.

The challenge of higher-level hockey is why the Junior Hockey experience is so valuable. After playing in the USHL, these boys will have a better understanding of what it means to a superior teammate and even a superior leader. The colleges and universities appreciate this experience for their young recruits as these boys show up on campus more ready to be impactful members of their college teams. They will bring with them a much better understanding of the concept of playing to win the game. No other major American college sport has a system like it.

ONE FRANCHISE LEADS THE WAY

For a period of years, when one looked at the rosters of Division I College and University Hockey Teams across America, alumni from ONE organization stood out more than most. That organization was our organization—the Sioux Falls Stampede. Our alumni on a yearly basis accounted for anywhere from three to four times more Division I University Captains than any other organization. That includes not just the 16-18 teams that compete in the USHL on a yearly basis, but junior teams from Canada and high school and prep teams across North America as well. The numbers verify that something special was going on in Sioux Falls. It is undeniable that what we were doing in Sioux Falls was impactful in the development and nurturing of leadership skills and the understanding of what it means to be a great teammate.

How our staff and I were able to nurture so many future collegiate leaders, and the various influences in helping me better understand leadership, is what this book is about. Those who through the years mentored and nurtured me indirectly impacted those whom I and our staff impacted in Sioux Falls. These young men today are in leadership positions elsewhere and are impacting others. The impact is exponential. This is why family and friends encouraged me over and again to write on this concept.

We are all products of many influences for sure, and I have been lucky to be exposed to many true leaders. While many of these stories revolve around the sport of hockey, the concepts are not limited to hockey. Leadership is a skill, which is an integral part of how to play and win at everything. The stories I relay in this book are about great teammates and what real-life leadership looks like. These are the skills our young people can and need to take into every team, from small teams like marriages to large corporate teams. We all need to be sure that our young people are being schooled on these important values in our free society. We all need to value and nurture these concepts and give more than lip service to their development.

CHAPTER 2:
FREEDOM IS OUR *WHY*

Why spend any time thinking about leadership? Freedom is why. This thing we in America have sought, this big concept of FREEDOM, it comes with a lot or responsibility. If we had a king telling us what to do, we wouldn't be free and we wouldn't need leadership, as it would be the king's job to lead. We in the masses would simply take whatever direction from the king and follow along, silently and obediently! Our nation's founding fathers didn't want that for us and for America. They believed in the individual's natural desire to be free. They believed in the individual's desire for self-determination.

Freedom, however, came with and continues to come with a price. Freedom requires much in the way of responsibility. We need to educate ourselves, be willing to work, be willing to lead as there is no king to do it for us. As each generation has progressed, I think we have more and more taken freedom for granted.

I have had the great fortune of coaching young people (ages 16-20) for many years now. These young people have shown me through our various interactions how much they take freedom for granted. I would say many in our society have become spoiled. They simply take for granted what opportunity they have each day as a free soul. They take for granted how great it is to get out of bed each morning with the world as one big opportunity. As my own kids have heard many times from me, *"today is the first day of the rest of your life!"*

Given the choice, however, many of these young people wouldn't get out of bed at all, at least not before noon. Because these young people awake to so much opportunity, they naturally take much of this for granted. I query my students as to their understanding of what freedom means, what makes a great leader and great teammate. They often do not know. They of course are young and have much to learn. We parents, teachers, coaches and mentors have a great opportunity to teach these young people. We as a free society need to work hard at constantly teaching and reinforcing the fundamentals of freedom and all that will be required to maintain all that has been built for us.

I remember fondly a Garfield (the cat) cartoon that made an impact on me. In the cartoon's first panel it shows the sometimes devious Garfield looking about the pet shop which includes many animals in cages. The next panel shows Garfield running in front of a row of cages, unlocking each cage as he goes along. In the third panel, all of the animals have stepped outside their respective cages finally free, but we can see by each in their expressions that they are perplexed with what to do next. Last panel, all the animals that were just freed from the bondage of their cages, jump back inside the cages to the safety of their individual *ruled-for-them* kingdoms. They chose to go back to a life of being fed and cared for. This is a great cartoon with a great message. While many of us revere freedom, freedom is scary to many others. Some would simply prefer to be taken care of. Our society has not been engineered that way—we revere freedom as a value, or at least we want to believe so.

A free society requires much in the way of leadership from its citizenry. A free society requires leadership in every walk of life. Freedom is fluid. Society can go in good directions and not so good directions. We have seen that in our history. We have led ourselves to some really good places but we have also allowed ourselves to go to some not so great places. But over time we have found a way to stick to the original vision for our country and fight for what is right and mostly, in the end we get it right. In order to continue on a healthy and prosperous path in America, the most free of societies, we need to continue to choose to nurture leadership by teaching its basic fundamentals.

FUNDAMETALS MATTER

We need to constantly acquaint ourselves with the fundamentals needed to operate a free society which many of us revere. As a many year hockey coach and manager of business teams, I know as most of you do the importance of sound fundamentals. Success in any endeavor requires a mastery of the basics. This is true whether it is in a sport, a branch of science, an academic undertaking or really any endeavor. A sound fundamental base is needed to move along to acquire higher levels of skills in that field.

We might all agree that, at times, we lose sight of what is important—to remain a free and prosperous republic. We need to make a commitment to keep the fundamentals of leadership in mind and we need to teach these fundamentals over and again to our up-and-coming generations of young people. When their Garfield lets them out of their cages, they need to be ready to embrace their freedom and not be afraid of it. Confidence comes from mastering the basics! And this is not just for their individual success, but also for ours as a country to remain just and free.

One can attend school to learn the fundamentals of many disciplines. Why is it that the fundamentals of leadership and becoming a great teammate are most often not offered as part of the menu of course selections? There are classes here and there, but to my knowledge, no college institution is offering a major in leadership. I spoke with a leader at a great American university who tells me he intends to change that. Why not offer a major in leadership? Why not leadership and the fundamentals of what it takes to be a great teammate? Outside of our military academies, we don't do much in the way of teaching the basics of great teamwork and leadership. Many of our marriages would be healthier if more had an understanding of these fundamentals. The same can be said for industrial teams, corporate teams and politics.

Should it then surprise any of us that time and time again, we all witness directly or through our various media, a lack of leadership at many levels? We all have to ask ourselves: Why? Why such a lack of leadership on so many levels in so many aspects of society? Maybe it is our fault as a society for not embracing and placing more focus on the teaching and nurturing of leadership principles. If we are to remain truly free, we need to reinforce these basic values. This book is my small way to simply re-start the conversation or refocus our efforts on leadership.

WHY—A BIG WORD WITH BIG IMPLICATIONS

When we were kids, we pestered our parents with questions of *why?* Kids naturally want to know *why* things are as they are. *Why* is our motivation for all we do and much of what we think. *Why* is why we get out of bed each morning. *Why* is the reason we start businesses and the reason our products sell. *Why* is the reason people join social movements. *Why* is the reason for all we do.

Our brain has a little file cabinet in it where we store our many *whys*. This is where our heartfelt feelings and motivations are safely kept and then released toward a goal of some kind. Though we say we feel it in our heart, it is really a part of our brain that gives us the drive and desire we need to accomplish a goal. When it comes to accomplishing goals, there is no more important concept. When teams of individuals share the same motivation, the same *why* for starting the project in the first place, the chances for success increase greatly. If you have ever been on one of those teams where the individuals are dedicated to the same team motivation and not just individual reward, well, it is truly a joy to go to work.

Unfortunately, we are living in a time where many of us in America have become cynical about lots of things. We are cynical because we too often don't understand *why* the other person thinks or acts the way they do. To be a cynic means that one is disinclined to recognize goodness or selflessness as a motive for behavior in others, and also one who takes a low view or even contempt of human behavior. Sounds like something I see on TV nightly. We often don't understand the motivation of our adversaries or politicians or a whole host of folks for what it is they do or say. We attribute a motivation, their *why* to something that is not so honorable.

Let's consider our political class. How often have you heard a friend or neighbor say something about not trusting our elected political leaders? And why should we trust our politicians when they don't trust each other? They often articulate a lack of trust in the motivations of one another and, in this regard, they have done much to damage our society. We have all heard it: *They just don't want poor people to benefit; they are just rich and greedy; they're just padding their own pockets.* I could go on and on with quotes by many who are considered leaders in our political class, but not to get personal here.

I suspect that most times, even the least skilled politicians want what it is they think is best for America. Unfortunately, too often we do not hear, "I know he wants what they think is best, but I think their idea might not be the best in this case because..." We don't hear that enough! Either many in our political class do not understand the why, the motivation of their opposition, or they just are too blind or unwilling to understand it.

When you see a real leader, you know it. A leader will most often understand the motivation of the opposing viewpoint. A leader may disagree with an opposing viewpoint or direction, but because s/he understands the opposing viewpoint and the motivations thereof, can be agreeable in the way they state their disagreement.

It is not that a politician disagrees with another that is bothersome and harmful to our society; it is in the way they often disagree. They tear each other down, with total distrust for one another in their words and actions. Unfortunately, this leads us to similar conclusions so we in turn do not trust. I don't believe many politicians really understand how much damage they do to the very culture they are elected to serve. It is desirable to dissent and debate in a free society. No one understands this better than real leaders. But the fundamentals of how we do so are extremely important.

Let's also consider the media. Our free society is watched over closely by what has been called the Fourth Estate (the first three estates of our society are one through three; 1-religion, 2-government, 3-the common man). This Fourth Estate is important to our freedom. A free media provides us with truth seeking. Their job is to help us free people see the world for what it is. They have a high level of responsibility in our free society.

Unfortunately, our Fourth Estate has seen better days as well. As it stands today, we can turn to different media outlets on the same day and it often appears that the story, the pursuit of the truth can be quite different from one outlet to another. I have seen many of the same stories reported by competing media outlets and, way too often, the stories are contradictory. At times it is hard to know what to believe. Our media outlets are supposed to help us navigate a complex world in the pursuit of the truth. They exist to educate us so we can make decisions that serve our free republic. They should rarely if ever get caught telling the story in half-truths or downright lies. But they do get caught…and we get more cynical.

Bad behavior continues in other disciplines and we become more cynical. Most of us saw or read reports of our secret service who were commissioned to protect our president in a foreign country. These are folks who we hold in high regard for their duty and obligation to protect our president and us. What could be a more important task than that of our basic protection? In the course of their duties, they as individuals and a group, allowed unprofessional behavior to happen in their rooms in a foreign country. In their misbehavior, they jeopardized their mission. In their lack of professionalism, in their lack of leadership and attention to detail to their main mission, they broke an oath to their duty and obligation to serve us and, maybe worse yet, they contributed to a further erosion of trust in our culture. What are our young people to think? What is any of us to think? I was left wondering…could one strong leader have led them down a better path?

I firmly believe in capitalism. All any of us need do is look at our country and see how far we have come in just over 250 years; it is amazing. Then not long ago the media informs us about scandals by leadership in the world's largest banks. Seemingly good folks within these banks were fixing the game, very small numbers it may have seemed, but in the large scale of what they do, it added up to a lot of money to these banks. Those inclined to distrust capitalism become further alienated by such reports, again leading to a cynical society. We need financial industry leaders who understand and take seriously the fundamentals of their duty and obligation to the *why* of why they exist. They have a duty to not just that task at hand, but to the society they are in business to serve.

I consider myself a conservative but my family is largely liberal. I love my family so I learn to love and appreciate their liberal viewpoint. I have found that my liberal family and I agree on plenty, we just often see different ways of getting to the same goal and that is a great debate of course. Then we turn on the TV and see leaders of each political party carry on our respective arguments but too often in ways that are counter-productive. They point fingers of blame and attribute opposing viewpoints to impure motivations. They purvey distrust in each other and consequently we in them. Many of us simply do not trust the system. We do not trust the money people to do what is right and prudent; we do not trust the political class to keep the money people in check: we do not trust, period. This cynicism is not good for the healthy conduct and growth of our continued pursuit of our free society.

We need to all agree as a free society that there is a real and serious obligation which burdens each of us in the continued pursuit of freedom and the advancement of our republic. Freedom is not now or will it ever be free. There is a price. We all know that many have sacrificed much for us. If freedom is to continue and even make positive strides, if we want to keep America great, this virtue, this pursuit is in all of our hands. Leaders and leadership needs to be nurtured. Leaders will need to rise and be heard and seen at every level of society. We cannot survive without great leadership. Great teams, great countries, great families and great corporate entities all need great leadership…and great teammates. And great leadership is like any other skill, it starts with fundamentals. Our society needs to take this leadership concept seriously.

LEADERS AND FREE SOCIETY

One of the more important fundamentals for a great functioning team, and a great functioning society, is that everyone needs to be a leader! We all need to understand that leadership comes in many shapes and sizes, with bigger roles on a team to smaller roles on a team.

Being a leader can be leading as little as one other person, or even just yourself. It starts with leading yourself, leading by example. You set the standard for yourself and if you set your standard high, others will want to follow. You can influence many by just being a good person and allowing others to see your goodness.

Setting a good example is a good start for leadership, but it often doesn't end there. Every one of us, from teen to adult, can identify with this one simple example. A friend or family member has had a couple of adult (alcoholic) beverages and shouldn't get in their car and drive. Because we love and care for this person and the others in our society out on the roads that could be put in danger as well, we do what is best for this person; we take the car keys away from them and/or line up a ride. We do whatever it takes to keep this loved one safe, not to mention the duty and obligation we have to keep others in our community safe on our roads. We enlist the help of others if we need to, but when it is time to lead, like in this drinking-and-driving scenario, it is time to lead. We may not have been selected or wanted to volunteer to be in that position at that moment in time, but when the moment arrives, it is time to lead.

We need to nurture these fundamental concepts in our young people. If our youngest generations are taught and allowed to practice and develop solid leadership and team building fundamentals, our society will improve in many ways. We will witness less drinking and driving fatalities at all ages. Society will produce better students, better parents, and better marriages, better everything. We as a society would set out on a rebranding campaign and no longer elect politicians, we would elect leaders. Wouldn't that be a nice change! Make no mistake, however, "it takes one to know one" if we want to recognize a leader when we see one, we need a society that knows what one looks like. Leadership needs to be a virtue by which we stand, because without it, we may fall.

Before I get on to real leadership in the real world, I would ask each person that reads this book to ask themselves what their definition of freedom is. Since freedom is why America exists, we should agree as to why we hold dear this virtue.

History reminds us that freedom was not a normal state of governance before we formed this great union, yet freedom is the natural state of being. Think about that. Each one of us if given the choice of being free or being a slave would choose freedom. Yet if freedom is our natural state of being and what we desire for our families, and ourselves, then maybe we ought to fully understand the fundamentals and obligations of being free. The animals in the Garfield cartoon wanted none of it because they were neither prepared nor equipped with the fundamentals skills needed to prosper outside their cages!

While we may have fought to not be ruled by a king, sometimes I think we are trading in the king for another king-like entity, a government king so to speak. Like the animals in the Garfield cartoon, some might prefer that the government king take care of us, especially since our growing cynical nature doesn't believe we can do it any other way. Trading in our freedom for governance that controls us is just another trade back to the days of a king. Trading our liberties for some kind of guarantee from the government king is not a wise direction for our free republic.

FUNDAMENTALS NEED PRACTICE

Since freedom is our number one virtue in our society, I looked up the word *virtue* in Webster's dictionary and found this definition: *a commendable quality*. I like that. Freedom is at minimum a commendable quality of the very fabric of our country, certainly one we have fought hard for. I also found as a definition of the word virtue, "a practice of duty." I don't know about you, but I find that quite profound. *Practice of duty* I take to mean the actual acts we employ. It is one thing to believe in something, it is another to act in accordance with those beliefs. So freedom is our commendable quality and is something we need to practice. But I would ask each of us, do we make freedom our profound quality, and do we teach and practice it?

It takes great practice at anything to become great, and it will take practice of duty to continue to be great at freedom. That seems a pretty big concept but like many skills or knowledge bases, it is not so big if one understands the basics. All fundamentals to any endeavor need positive practice and learning! The question that hits me as a member of this great and free United States is: Are we teaching how to practice this duty, this obligation to freedom?

I know there are ethics classes in college. Maybe that suffices for some, but I do not believe that is near enough society wise. Do we really believe in this "practice of duty"? Do our young people truly understand what burdens they inherit in a free society? Each generation must pay the price and hopefully not in blood like so many before us and currently in our armed forces. We can and need to do a better job teaching and practicing our duty to freedom.

I have been fortunate to work with young people. I often ask them what freedom means to them. After hearing many of their answers, I believe that for understandable reasons, they take freedom for granted. Why wouldn't they? They mostly don't know any different. I also don't think they really understand freedom. They have little perspective with which to compare.

I tried to define freedom for myself. As is my preference, I like to first go to the dictionary, but in this case, I cannot find a definition that is in my mind complete. There are definitions about free of slavery to others or free to choose or free to make decisions. Those are all a good start and part of the definition for sure, but they don't totally work for me. I believe the freedom we sought in our great revolution has another element. It has the element of consequences.

Yes, we are free to make choices, free of interference from others, but it also comes with the freedom to experience the consequences of those decisions. Do we decide to get educated or not, to spend our money wisely or waste it, to be kind or not, to act safely or dangerously? In all cases, freedom in my opinion means we get to reap the rewards from good decisions and suffer the consequences of our bad decisions.

Freedom has lots of added responsibilities and that is why the animals freed by Garfield jumped back in their cages. While they were suddenly free to determine their own future and no longer a captive or slave to another, they all suddenly began to think about where the next meal was coming from. To take care of one's own self and those we care about is real freedom and I believe, like in the Garfield cartoon, it is scary for many. Weren't we all a bit scared when we left our home as young adults, off into the world, *free*…

In all my years of coaching, the only solution I found to counteract fear and lack of confidence was *working very hard on the fundamentals until they were mastered!* Then when one was let out from the cage and put in the game, they had a real chance for success!

In summary, I believe, as I know many of you do as well, that freedom comes with a set of responsibilities and values that we need to embrace, practice and reinforce. We cannot cower and allow others to care for us if we truly embrace freedom. But, like the Garfield cartoon some are afraid of freedom and are too often allowing and even preferring others to make decisions and care for them. America isn't the best place for them.

I have fallen in love with history. There is so much to be learned from history and for me, time and again, history reminds me of the important fundamental values that we are blessed with in America. Recently I re-watched a movie I think is a great movie and great history lesson, *Amistad*. If you haven't seen it, it is both an incredible true story and also an incredibly well made movie. Directed by Steven Spielberg, and to my novice understanding of acting, I would call the acting superb. The movie is of pre-civil wartime and tells the story of a group of Africans who are stolen from their African homeland and sold into slavery. They were being transported on the Spanish ship, La Amistad. In their quest to regain their freedom they revolted and took control of the ship, a ship they had no expertise in navigating. After taking control of the ship, they wandered aimlessly until they wound up just off the shore of Connecticut in the relatively young United States of America. At the time the United States still acknowledged and utilized the slave trade.

There is a great oration in the movie delivered by Academy Award winning actor Sir Anthony Hopkins, who plays the role of John Quincy Adams, then former president of the United States. The former president presented the case on behalf of the Africans to the US Supreme Court. The movie is worth watching just for Sir Anthony Hopkins oration to the Supreme Court. The movie provides a great history lesson for sure and a great chance for all of us to revisit the very basic concept of freedom and what it should mean to every human being.

America's stated values were that of freedom and liberty. The Africans who fought for their freedom on *La Amistad* helped America find justice in our long-standing fight for freedom. They were part of America's journey to a justice for all. The movie tells this story and the legal battles that ensued which in a large part led to the outbreak of the United States Civil War. These Africans in the end were not looked upon as property of the slave trade but human beings with a natural right to fight for freedom. If you haven't seen the movie, it is well worth your time.

In the end, I believe freedom is to be free of a king or slave-owner and brings with it the opportunity to wake up each and every day and make decisions, make choices on what kinds of actions one will take. Good actions and good decisions are most often rewarded and poor decisions and poor actions will be most often punished. One can get out of bed, work hard, treat people well and so on or one can choose not to. Like any coach or manager would tell his team, the more good decisions the individual and team make, the better the chances of success. In our society, no one is there to do it for us.

In the end, to remain truly free, we need leaders in every part of our society. To be just, to live in a free society in a way that is with honor and integrity, we need real leaders who lead with love and respect. We do not in theory want or accept that the king, the slave owner or the government feed and clothe us, tell us how to do or what to do daily; that is up to each of us in a free society. To do that well, we need to educate our young, direct and role model for our young. We need to provide and produce and prosper on our own and for our own, not for the king, the slave owner nor the government. That, in my opinion, was the value of freedom that our great country was founded upon and the value we must continue to work hard to keep and nurture. Freedom simply brings with it much more responsibility to which we all need to be accountable and continue to nurture. Many have died to provide us this opportunity. We need to do a better job as a society in teaching and nurturing the responsibilities that come with being able to live in this great and free society.

CHAPTER 3:
MY ROOTS IN LEADERSHIP

I grew up in St. Paul, Minnesota. St. Paul was and still is today a very good baseball town. Major League all-stars were coming out of St. Paul, guys like Jack Morris, Paul Molitor, Dave Winfield and more recently, Joe Mauer. Our St. Paul city conference was a solid baseball conference. Statistically, I was a much more impactful player in high school baseball than I was in high school hockey. I had some college baseball scouts come and watch me play, visit practice to time me on the base paths, doing the things and saying the things college scouts do. It's nice to be acknowledged for your ability but the fact remained that I loved hockey.

I will always love the energy of the game of hockey. I love the duty and obligation of being a hockey teammate…a teammate one can count on to do the job when the game of hockey gets hard. I love the code of honor in hockey and how the players know the code without it seemingly ever been formally taught to them. I love how hockey players sacrifice for one another, how they sleep and eat for each other, how they stand shoulder to shoulder together, and often in adverse situations.

The game will test you and your teammates on many levels and especially those levels that involve character and courage. The few endeavors I can imagine that might create a stronger bond of brotherhood might be within the tight knit families of the military or fire department, where your safety and even your lives depend on each other. In hockey, a life isn't on the line, but often one's well-being is. Players stick together no matter what.

Hockey is a sport and life I aspired to. I turned down a baseball scholarship to pursue hockey. I tried out for the St. Paul Vulcans of the old Midwest Junior Hockey League and was fortunate to make the team. The St. Paul Vulcans were, and still are today in my mind, the Grand-Daddy of Junior Hockey in America.

Back in the late 1960s, a group of hockey leaders concerned with development of local hockey talent saw a real missing link in hockey's development chain. They knew that hockey was a world sport and all other countries allowed their developing players to remain in development until the age of 20. In Minnesota, with high school hockey being the predominant developing grounds for its players, players remained *in development* only until the age of 18. At 18 it was off to college or, for many, be done with the game they so loved.

So these hockey leaders and pioneers formed the Midwest Junior Hockey League. This allowed players like me to play through their high school career and if not ready for college or professional hockey, we still had a couple of years of development time remaining in Junior Hockey. Guys like me could take advantage of the best of both the high school and Junior Hockey experience.

The St. Paul Vulcan franchise and Midwest Hockey League always played second-fiddle to all the other levels of hockey in Minnesota. The Minnesota hockey community really didn't understand Junior Hockey. They knew and understood only a very well established system of high school hockey. Crowds and supporters for a Midwest Junior Hockey League game in Minnesota were small, often just family members, friends and a few scouts. Still, for teams like the Vulcans, there were expenses to pay.

I really don't know how the Vulcan founders and leadership managed financially. It had to be only that so many great hockey people were willing to work together to find a way. The organization was led by Ron Woodey, Harry Sundberg, Bob Somers, Dr. Harry Brown and many more including the help of coaches like Herb Brooks and Doug Woog. Many put in their time, others put in their money. It was a saving grace for guys like me.

The consequences of these pioneers' great work was that many young people, including me,were afforded the additional development time needed to achieve hockey scholarships to the many hockey-playing colleges and universities in America. With each passing year the value of the league to its participants increased. The league was becoming a real source of talent for America's colleges and universities and eventually the NHL.

I graduated from St. Paul Washington High School in 1976. That next fall I tried out for and made the 1976-77 version of the St. Paul Vulcans. I might add that I barely made the team. I didn't play much the first half of that first year in St. Paul. I was finding out about the toughness part of the game…what toughness was and what it wasn't. I wasn't very tough. I was a relatively nice boy who loved to compete and this league and my coaches were showing me the way of things. For me, it didn't come quick and it didn't come easy.

About 25 games into my first season of Junior Hockey with the Vulcans we had played our final game before Christmas break at the Bloomington Ice Gardens against the Bloomington Junior Stars. Head Coach Doug Woog, who would eventually go on to coach at the University of Minnesota, was quite upset with us because of our lack of focus. In our locker room after the game, Coach Woog went around the room criticizing each of us for our lack of focus in the game just played and also for many of our faults he had witnessed in the first half of the year. Some of it was pretty harsh individual criticism.

As coach Woog made his rounds, I sat there thinking to myself: *When that finger he is pointing comes around to me, what can he possibly criticize me about…I hardly play*! As Coach Woog's index finger finally came around to me for my turn, I saw the point of his index finger hit me right between the eyes as he said, looking me straight in the eyes, "Hartzell, you're lucky you don't bitch or you wouldn't be here." That's an exact quote! Wow, I think there is a whole story that could be told in that little critique from Coach Woog.

Fact is, I didn't bitch or complain, but I also hadn't yet proved to him that I had what it took to play regularly at this level or certainly beyond. I was happy to be part of this team but obviously had some improving to do and while we maybe were not the greatest team at that point in time, we were about to get better and eventually win the Anderson Cup, awarded to the team with the best record throughout the regular season. I was about to get better too!

A LEADER STEPS UP

Getting over the hump to the point where I was a dependable everyday player was my personal challenge. How was I to get to that point? I was fortunate to be led, not just by a good coach in Doug Woog, but also by a good friend on the team by the name of Frank Serratore. Frank was our main goalie and somehow took a liking to me (years later he would joke that he really was more interested in my sister Annette and her group of high school girlfriends that we would run across from time to time). Frank took time to lead me in the right direction. He was a leader then and is a leader today.

Today Frank Serratore is the head hockey coach at the Air Force Academy. Frank, in my opinion, has done as good a job of coaching his college program as any hockey coach in America. His Air Force team often makes the NCAA Tournament and does so without being able to recruit the very best top pure hockey talent. What he does get are good hockey players who also want to be Air Force Cadets. I am very proud of him. Frank is from Coloraine, Minnesota, a small town on Minnesota's Iron Range where hockey is big. Baseball was big there too and in later years Frank and I would play some town-ball baseball together also. I am a better person and player for having Frank in my life.

In 1976, Frank was our number one Vulcan goaltender. Frank had a unique view of my abilities, especially in practice. That was good because I wasn't playing in the games very much. He knew that I had at least some of the important building blocks it takes to be a good player. He encouraged me but he also told me the way things were. I still remember a game where Frank was not playing. That means that as the games back up goalie, he was sitting on the bench....with me! He must have seen some frustration on my face, as I wasn't playing much in the game...again. On the bench during the game he leaned over to me and said, "Wooger knows you're a good player but you need to get tougher in the corners." I respected Frank. Who wanted to hear anything negative much less that I had to get tougher? But I didn't resist his advice; I listened. I learned later that when Coach Woog asked Frank for his advice about who to keep during some late cuts to the team's roster, Frank had told him, "I'd keep Hartzell...he does a lot of good things as a hockey player and scores a lot in practice."

Leaders need to and will give honest feedback as they see it. Frank gave me honest assessment, honest feedback of my abilities, and he led me when I needed leading. He was what I needed; he was mindful of what was going on around him. He was mindful of my needs. He gave me exactly what I needed when I needed it; honest assessment from a person in my life that I in turn knew cared about me.

With Frank's encouragement I was about to make a step forward. My patience and work ethic were about to be rewarded. When the second half of the season got under way, I was going to get my chance and when it came, I made the most of it. After scoring just two goals before Christmas, I ended the season on the team's top scoring line with 18 regular season goals and led the whole league in scoring in the play-offs. It was quite the positive change for the guy who was lucky to be on the team because he didn't "bitch".

Steve Ulseth was a late-season addition to our roster. Steve started the season playing high school hockey for his hometown high school, Kellogg High in Roseville, MN. He joined our team in February after his team lost in the high school play-offs. His addition to our roster was a positive boost for both me and the team. We were put together as line-mates and to this day, he is the player I played with in my career with whom I had the best chemistry. I seemed to know what he was thinking and he seemed to know the same of me.

Once joined on a line together, along with Jim Mrozak of St. Paul Johnson (a future Ohio State Buckeye), we scored a lot. I scored a lot. It was almost magical the chemistry we had together. This chemistry brought out the best in me. In the most important late-season game against our main regular season rival, Lou Vairo's Austin Mavericks, our line scored all five goals in a 5-4 win with me getting three of the goals. We clinched the Anderson Cup, the USHL regular season championship. As I walked out of the locker room after that game, Coach Woog winked at me and said with his wry smile, "I should have cut you when I had the chance!" He of course was joking about the very fact that he had considered such a move at the beginning of the year. It seemed he had made the right choice in keeping me. It was a very gratifying moment for me.

After winning the regular season championship, we went all the way through the play-offs before losing game seven of the final series to the Bloomington Jr. Stars. You never want to lose the play-off championship in hockey. The play-offs in Junior Hockey are played as multiple-game series just like the pros and there is no more fun experience in hockey than making a long run the in play-offs. We did well but finished one game short of a play-off championship. Taking the season in its entirety, it had to be considered a very successful year by all involved in the Vulcan organization. And for me, personally, I had come a long ways.

I received a hand-written note in the mail from legendary U of Minnesota head coach Herb Brooks congratulating me on my progress throughout the year along with a reminder to keep working to get better. Coach Brooks was also a St. Paul native and I think he felt a kinship to St. Paul kids and wanted to see them advance in hockey.

My Vulcan coach Doug Woog became my biggest advocate and after the season ended, his work and leadership on my behalf got me included in the regional tryout for the United States World Junior Team. The regional camp was at the Bloomington Ice Gardens. Considering that at the start of the 1976 season I wasn't even playing much on a junior team, to be at the regional camp was proof I had made great progress as a player. Most the invitees were already 18/19-year-old college and university players. Just to be there was an honor and a testament to the progress I had made. Then a funny thing happened, I made it thru that regional trial and was invited to the final tryout which took place in late summer in Colorado Springs, Colorado.

This tryout at the United States Olympic Training Center was another in the many turning points in my career and really in my life. I went there thinking I had almost no chance to make the team. As I looked around at the other players, some of which I knew and looked up to, I was looking mostly at players already playing NCAA Division I hockey. Most had just completed their freshman year of college. They didn't need Junior Hockey like I did. They were highly talented and were able to go the traditional route back then, right from high school to college. They had greater reputations than I. I didn't even as yet have a college hockey commitment. I had only a handwritten note from Herb Brooks to keep on striving for more.

I played my game throughout the tryout, which is what every player should do in a tryout: just play your game to the best of your ability. I must have done pretty well because I would later be told I was the number one pick for the team of all the forwards in the camp. I still cannot believe that. I made the darn US World Junior Team! Representing my country in a World Tournament, and in my opinion, one of the very best tournaments of any kind in the world, will always be a highlight of my life.

Before the World Junior Tournament would begin at Christmastime of the next season, I would start my second season of Junior Hockey with the Vulcans. This particular season would involve a merger; the Midwest Junior League and the professional United States Hockey League (USHL). The old USHL was a semi-professional league and inhabited such cities as Green Bay and the Iowa cities of Sioux City, Des Moines and Waterloo. This particular year would begin a transition from what was a professional league to an all amateur junior league. Professional USHL teams were required to roster just six junior-aged amateur players in year one (1977) of the merger. That meant while each of these teams would field a minimum of 6 junior-aged players, they also had another 15 plus players that were professionals. This was going to be quite the challenge for our traditional junior teams.

If today's USHL is a rugged and competitive league, that 1977 version was even more so! A game early in that season in Green Bay again changed the way I looked at the game. Early in that game I was screening the goaltender (standing right in front of him to take away his vision for stopping the puck), and back in those days it took some courage to stand in front of the other team's goaltender. Back then players would take liberties on anyone standing in front of their goalie, meaning you were going to get black and blue from the opponent's sticks being laid not so gently on your arms, ribs and ankles.

I felt a heavy and painful smack to my ankles. I looked back to see the Green Bay goaltender taking another whack at me. I took exception with the Green Bay goalie taking liberties on me. As play came to a halt, a minor confrontation between the goalie and I took place. The Green Bay players came to the defense of their goalie as teams do. No team then or now allows anyone to touch or confront their goalie. Nothing really came of that altercation. Well; not yet anyway.

Just a few minutes later I came down the slot with the puck, the slot being the scoring area directly in front of the goalie, and let my best shot rip. Just as I shot, the puck wobbled a bit and instead of going where I was trying to shoot it, it went up at a pretty steep angle and hit the goalie right between the eyes. He was knocked totally unconscious! While I didn't try to do it, it happened and just a moment after that previous altercation. Everyone, and especially the Green Bay team, thought I did it to retaliate for the liberties he took on me. Keep in mind the goalie masks were not so good back then. Anyone who knows me knows I don't shoot the puck that hard in any circumstance so it must have been a real primitive mask! I remember even some of my teammates saying to me "wow, Hartzy, that took some balls to give it to him like that!" Everyone, even my own teammates thought I did it on purpose!

Like any hockey team would do, the Green Bay guys came to their goalie's defense and many of my teammates came to mine. I was a marked man for the remainder of that game and the next night. But I learned something that night: I played well a bit scared. You can call it scared, you can call it aware, but I knew those Green Bay guys were trying to put more into every hit, every time I skated by someone I got a stick. But I also realized then that I played better with this new heightened awareness. I also came to better understand the value of a real team. My team was there for me. I had 20 allies out there, all for one and one for all! It is a great feeling to have great teammates who are with you through thick and thin.

That night the USHL tested my teammates and me, and together we passed the test. And I got better! That's what a great league does, it tests you in new ways and you either pass the test or you go home and complain to your parents that the coaches are not good enough or some such excuse that many conjure up to protect their egos. I think I passed the test and went on to have a good first half of the season before leaving for a couple of weeks at Christmastime for the World Junior Tournament.

The World Junior Tournament is one of the finest tournaments of any kind in the world. Held annually at Christmastime, it is a tournament that resembles the Olympics. Each nation sends its best hockey players under the age of 20 to a different world location each year for this great spectacle of hockey talent. The tournament is attended by every NHL team and its top scouts as many of the world's best NHL draft-eligible players come to one location.

Back then the best teams year in and year out were the Soviet Union, Czechoslovakia, Sweden, Finland and of course Canada. The United States wasn't quite yet being taken that seriously on the world stage, certainly nowhere near where it is today. Game one for me and my USA teammates was in the old Montreal Forum against a powerful Team Canada who fielded their usual outstanding team. Team Canada had future NHL Hall-of-Famers like Wayne Gretzky, Mike Gartner, Rick Vaive and many others who populated this team. Longtime

Forum anthem singer Roger Doucet came out and sang the Anthems in both English and French, something I had seen on TV many times. Roger Doucet singing the anthems were a WOW moment for me!

We didn't beat Team Canada in that first game of the tournament, but we gave them a scare. After falling behind 3-0, we rallied tying the game 3-3 in the third period. Finally Team Canada awoke and beat us 6-3. I was just smart enough to grab a score-sheet after the game for a memento which I still have.

In hindsight, I cannot even imagine how much pressure that Canadian team had to feel in that game. A kid like Gretzky was only 16 at the time and their whole team was of course under the age of 20. Representing their hockey-crazed country on home ice in the historic Montreal Forum in what was also game 1 for them against an inferior U.S team had to be difficult. The US may be on equal footing with Canada today, but back then, Canada was the superior hockey program. As young kids in that environment the pressure they carried on their shoulders had to be heavy. They had their whole country's expectations on their shoulders and losing to the USA back then would have been very much unacceptable. In the end their superior talent prevailed.

Our US team did fine throughout the tournament. We lost to Canada and Czechoslovakia and beat Switzerland and Germany. We were relegated to the consolation round which we won. In the Consolation Championship game against Finland we won by a score of 7-6. It was a great and entertaining game in front of a Canadian crowd clearly rooting against us and for the Fin's.

I was fortunate that our coach Len Lilyholm did his homework. He knew of the chemistry developed the year before with the Vulcans between myself and Steve Ulseth who at the time was a freshman at the University of Minnesota. We were put together on the same line throughout the tournament and continued our strong and positive chemical reaction. We continued where we had left off the year before with the Vulcans. I finished the tournament as one of the team's leading scorers; second I believe. Being uncommitted to any college and also being a very solid student, the fun was about to begin. For a kid who thought he was simply a pretty good baseball player, I was about to be a highly recruited college hockey prospect. I showed on the world stage that I could hold my own as a player and contribute on the scoring front as well. Playing well in front of so many scouts…well, that's how word travels in the hockey industry.

Since then, one too many times I have seen a young person not pursue their passion. That to me is most always a mistake. Maybe like me with a possible baseball future, they have a financial incentive to do something other than their passion. I chose my passion. While I did not come from a family with means, saying no to baseball could have been viewed by others to not be financially wise. But I had a good family who understood my passion. Pursuing what I was really passionate about will always be my first really good decision in life.

PART TWO: REAL-WORLD LEADERSHIP

CHAPTER 4:
TWO INFLUENTIAL LEADERS: MY DAD AND LEGENDARY HOCKEY COACH HERB BROOKS

If indeed it does take one to know one, what do we need to know that we could recognize a leader if we saw one? What do these leaders actually look like? Do they have special horns growing from their heads or walk a certain way? Most certainly they likely look like anyone and everyone else, but they do have plenty of characteristics that separate them from *the pack* of same-way thinkers. What separates them from *the pack* is just that they aren't afraid to be themselves; they listen, they learn and they make decisions that are often mindfully different than *the pack*. But always, they base their decisions on knowledge and values. They know growth and improvement is an ongoing pursuit. They know new paths and ways of doing things are always in their future.

I grew up with a high-end leader for a dad. As a kid I hadn't yet come to understand and recognize all the fundamentals of leadership, so I didn't truly realize what a leader my father was until sometime post high school. My dad was for a time president of Iron Workers Union Local #512. Anyone who knows anything about the building trade unions in the Upper Midwest knows that the iron workers are one tough bunch of guys. They worked hard and some played pretty hard too. Folks from outside the union wouldn't want to mistakenly or willingly be taking or infringing on their union work. Such behavior would likely warrant a visit from someone from the union to have a little conversation about who would be doing what in the future. If these conversations needed a little physical message for reinforcement, then so be it. Their methods weren't always "politically correct" but it was and continues to be a strong brotherhood for sure. They took care of their brothers and their families.

My dad Eugene, Gene or Geno most people called him, was a lifelong DFL'er, a supporter of the Democratic Farm Labor Party (political party). He always felt the DFL stood by the *little guy* as he referred to the everyday American worker. He felt strongly that the *little guy* needed advocates in the various political arenas. Along with the DFL, they had to be united in the fight for what was needed in society. My dad was one of those guys in the fight for the common man. Unions had to fight the *big money* and influence of corporate America and stand together for better working conditions. And a union man he was!

My dad was a youth in the Great Depression. When his father vanished, a mystery to this very day, he quit school in the eighth grade to go to work to help his family through the hard times of the Depression. Current generations can barely conceive of a child quitting formal education before high school. If a child quit school in the eighth grade in today's world with the willing support of his/her immediate family, someone from child welfare services would be making a visit to investigate such "child neglect". But this was the 1930s and families did what they needed to do. So too did the young man who was to become my father.

Still a young man and already with a number of years in the adult working world to provide for his family, my dad was summoned to serve his country in World War II like many young men of his age. He was part of an artillery unit that did their thing throughout France and Germany. He never boasted nor complained about his service to his country or family. There was no whining about losing his youth or innocence lost. Well, he did complain about the country of France not fighting in World War II. He said more than once that if it wasn't for the United States and our fighters, the French would be "speaking German". We did not hear any of his war stories until we had kids of our own and our kids would ask grandpa about his wartime experiences. When our kids asked *Grandpa* is when we finally heard some of his WW II stories.

Mostly what I knew of my dad was that he worked hard every day. Like good teammates do in hockey, he earned the respect of his rugged union brothers one day at a time. He was part of an extended brotherhood of men supporting their families throughout the Twin Cities area and the region. These men would leave home for months at a time to places like Alaska to work the iron workers trade. If lucky enough to be on the job, there would be no family vacations as work time was too valuable. If temporarily out of a job most families couldn't afford a family vacation. We almost didn't know what a family vacation was.

This brotherhood of iron workers took their job seriously and their union brotherhood was their loyal bond. My dad could be uncompromising because he had developed through mindful attention to detail what *right* and *wrong* looked like. And for him, there was only one way to do something and that was the right way. A person learns their trade and there is a right way to do things. He held everyone accountable to do the same. Contractors who hired the union labor owed his union brothers for their labor, but his union brothers also owed their employers an "honest day's work for an honest day's pay." He said that many more than a few times.

My brother-in-law Mike Walters also made his living as an iron worker. He tells a great story about how on one of his very first jobs as a young apprentice iron worker, he and another *newbie* showed up on the job site where my dad was also working. No sooner had my dad set eyes on these two youngsters, than did he see that something wasn't right with these two. My dad saw that their tool belts were not totally and properly equipped. As Mike tells it, my dad wasted no time sending both of the youngsters back to the Union Hall and told them both there was no room for not having it right. He was sure to let them know that they owed it to the job and their profession and to the folks paying them to have prepared better. Mike, in telling the story, said it was a great lesson for him to start his career and that everyone knew that my dad would hold all accountable. Good leaders always have a way of holding everyone around them accountable.

It was this honorable approach to all that mattered, to his profession and everyone involved in his profession that led his union brothers to elect him more than once to be their president. Labor strife and strikes came and went. Visitors of union brothers from other cities came to our house to visit. This may be overstating this a bit but it always seemed a bit to me like a movie where the *crime family* has private meetings where their plans are not to be heard by anyone outside of *the family*. They were family, to that there was no doubt and my father was one of their leaders.

I shall never forget old Geno's stubborn conversation with a St. Paul police officer in the front room of our very small home on Cottage Avenue in St. Paul. My dad had called the police to our home to report a threat he had received. What led up to the police officer being in our home was a late summer night street fight that happened right out in front of our residence. The friends of one of the participants had come back to the scene trying to find out more about what had happened to their good friend that had left him in the hospital. We came to suspect that their hospitalized friend, who we believe picked the fight in the first place, wanted to save face while he lay in the hospital so he told his friends that there had been a party at this house (our house) and a gang of fellas came out of the house and did this bodily damage to him. My dad had heard the skirmish the night before, but really didn't know exactly what had happened. He knew only that there were two fellas going at it pretty good.

I didn't see the conversation my dad had with these fellas when they showed up at our front door. I just remember my mom telling me how my dad just had to be my dad and not back down from the truth, telling these guys at our front door of our home about what had happened the previous night. He told them that their friend likely was fibbing to them to save his macho image as there was no party at our house or anywhere in the neighborhood, only a one-on-one fight out front. My mom told me that these guys became agitated with my dad and told him they would check for a few more "facts", but that our home might get a re-visit that night. My dad didn't take too kindly to being threatened.

I did get to see the next scene. It was a St. Paul police officer in our front room. The officer was saying to my dad, "Gee, Mr. Hartzell, you can't just go and shoot somebody just cause they come in your yard." My dad replied, "I'm not asking you about what I can do, I'm telling you that these guys threatened our home and family and if they step foot in my yard tonight, I'm going to shoot em". Being the avid outdoorsman and hunter he was, he had the guns to do so. "But Mr. Hartzell", the cop started to reply, when my dad cut him right off saying, "Hey, I'm not asking you anything, I'm telling you what I'm going to do. So if you don't want them getting shot, you might want to keep them out of my yard!"   We sat up that warm summer night, brother-in-law Mike Walters joining us, windows open with the window screens allowing all the breeze and noise into the house, lights turned down, with shotguns and shotgun shells at the ready. A St. Paul Police patrol car cruised by seemingly every five minutes or so throughout the night. It was a peaceful but interesting night. Nothing more ever came of the incident.

A couple of years later when the call came to inform me and my family that I was the number one pick as a forward out of the US Junior camp in Colorado Springs, it was one of my parents who answered the phone. I wasn't home. The voice on the other end of the phone told my parents the good news of my selection to the team but because only a part of the team was being named out of the summer tryout camp, others would be added as the new season progressed; the news was not for publication. The entire team would be "officially" named in early December. Well, my parents decided not to even tell me. My dad would tell me later that they thought it best I not get distracted and remain focused on what I was doing with my Vulcan Junior team and just keep working for that college deal I was working so hard for.

I had a part-time job at JC Penny. One early December morning in the break room I read in the *St. Paul Pioneer Press* that the US Junior National team had been named and to my excitement, I was listed as making the team. I immediately called home to share the news with my parents and was told by my mom who answered my call that both she and dad had known since that phone call they received a couple of months back. I couldn't believe it. Who does that? You know who does that...my parents. When they received that call that late summer day, they didn't go and boast to friends or even family to boost their own egos. It wasn't about them. I am certain they were proud and happy for me, but they didn't even tell me! They did what they thought was best for me...that I think is leadership...putting the best interests of others in front of yours!

My dad loved watching hockey. It was his love of hockey that introduced me to the game. Yet he didn't even attend the World Junior Tournament to watch his son play. Maybe it was financial, maybe work related, I don't recall. But he did say more than once, as I made my way throughout my hockey travels from younger ages to older, that this hockey adventure was mine and not his. He supported me in many ways. He came to more of my games than anyone else, but not all and not the World Junior Tournament. I will always respect that attitude of his as I know his actions were in fact what he thought was best for his son, not for a dad's ego.

Down deep, I knew my dad was an honorable man and a leader. That said, I think all us sons and daughters take our parents for granted at some level. What we see in and of our parents is mostly what we think everyone has. We think what our parents have and do is everyday normal. Looking back, I know I was lucky to have him as a father and a strong moral role model. There is no question that the most important leaders in our life are our parents. Leadership I think has to be part of my DNA but, in the end, I had great role models in my parents. My kids may not know it, but in me, they often are getting a good dose of Grandma and Grandpa.

HERBIE—A LEADER FOCUSED ON SERVING OTHERS

Leaders lead for sure but leaders also will follow if they know you have their best interest at the forefront of all you do.

Leaders will be not self-focused, but focused on what's good for the group and its individual members. When you meet a real leader and you know they are looking out for you, one will often choose to follow!

It was soon after my good performance in the World Junior Tournament that Herb Brooks, then U of Minnesota Head Hockey Coach and legendary U S hockey coach called, and invited me to visit the U of Minnesota campus. He walked me around campus personally and I felt a bond to my elder St. Paul native. I don't recall being at all intimidated by him. Under his leadership, the Golden Gophers had won two National Championships in his 7-year tenure, so I guess I should have felt some kind of intimidation, but I don't think I did.

He again had a strong team that particular year. I was just starting to believe I could play at such a quality program as Minnesota. Things were about to get interesting. Coach Brooks was about to do one of the classiest things I have seen in my time in sports and only a confident leader would do such a thing.

I think Herbie felt a special kinship with me as I was a St. Paul native like he. St. Paul had hockey players develop for the Division I levels, but not many and certainly not many on to the U of Minnesota. In my neighborhood, going to the University of Minnesota and playing for the Gophers would be viewed as the ultimate achievement. It would have been easy for Herbie to call me in and overwhelm me with the opportunity of playing there. He did not.

Herbie knew I was a very good student and that after the World Junior Tournament I suddenly was a "hot prospect". I was receiving letters and phone calls from Ivy League schools like Dartmouth and Brown, from tech-engineering schools like Michigan Tech and from schools out west like Colorado College. I was already scheduled to go on my first official recruiting visit to University of Northern Michigan.

When Herbie called me in for this official visit at the U of MN we had a great talk about life and what was important. I remember a general message from Herbie about my academics and a bright future if I kept striving for better. Before I left his office, Herbie handed me a yellow piece of paper that he signed (which I still have), which said that the U of Minnesota was committing a scholarship to me. That piece of paper would serve as a personal insurance policy of sorts. He didn't want a commitment to the university from me; at least not yet. He was however making a commitment from the university to me! He told me that being an excellent student and knowing the Ivies and others were starting the recruiting process with me, that I owed it to myself to get out and see what these other schools had to offer. He knew I was a sheltered St. Paul kid who before the World Junior experience, had never so much as been on an airplane. It was a different world then, pre-internet. Kids like me didn't know much about anything outside of our immediate eyesight. I certainly didn't know much at all about these other colleges and the opportunities they had to offer.

I had much to learn and consider. He afforded me the time to do so, to explore my options and make a decision that best suited my future. That is rare, very rare in the college recruiting game, especially today. As a many year Junior Hockey coach, I have witnessed many times over how the various schools and their recruiters work to get kids committed to their institutions. It is nothing like Herbie's approach.

Today the recruiting game is very competitive. Young assistant coaches are evaluated on their ability to land good and even great recruits. In my case, Herb himself did the final leg-work and I think Herb really did put my interests ahead of everything else. I cannot be anything but grateful and respect his great leadership, which in this case was a true concern for someone else. It was his true concern for me.

Well, explore I did. My final four schools that I was considering attending were Dartmouth, Michigan Tech, Colorado College and Minnesota. I could not have made a bad choice. No school tried harder than Dartmouth. Loyal alums would call to educate me on their great institution and they had current and former players from Minnesota who also called to attest to the quality of the Dartmouth experience. I have no doubt that Dartmouth would have been a great choice for me.

At the time, I felt Minnesota had no equal on the hockey side of the equation. Dartmouth made a Final Four appearance during my four-year career as did Michigan Tech who we actually beat in a Final Four semi-final my junior year. I really didn't make up my mind until a day or two before signing day. It wasn't because of Herb's concern for me that I chose Minnesota, I just weighed all the factors and the fact was, at least in my eyes, I wanted to play within the best hockey program possible. And back then it was the Minnesota Gophers. I wanted a great education and Minnesota provided that as well. But it could have been one of the other schools too. I was lucky to be led by a good man and great leader in Coach Brooks. His accomplishments are legendary and I was fortunate to be part of the Golden Gopher family.

During my freshman year at Minnesota, as we trained and were to eventually win the NCAA National Championship, Herbie's third National Championship, I heard Herbie say that he graduated from Minnesota with a major in Psychology. When I heard him say it, I knew at that very moment, I was going to be a Psychology major and future coach also. Leaders inspire. Leaders teach lessons that get handed down from one generation to the next. I was and continue to be inspired by Herbie and many others to lead with integrity and service to others.

Years later when I was coaching in Sioux Falls, I had a player by the name of Matt Lindblad from Chicago who was committed to Dartmouth. Matt likely still doesn't know that Herb Brooks had an influence on his career path. A Dartmouth staff member told me they intended to leave Matt with us for a third year of juniors. I disagreed with their direction and put forth a pretty strong argument that they owed it to Matt to bring him in to Dartmouth the very next year. Like Herbie did with me, I argued on behalf of Matt who was totally ready to attend college emotionally and especially as a hockey player.

I reasoned to the Dartmouth staff that while I would take Matt back with our Junior team in a heartbeat, we all would be holding him back if we had him play another year of juniors. While our team might benefit, we would not be doing Matt a service. In the end, Matt went to Dartmouth that very next year and led the entire team in scoring as a freshman. He proved me right. His career development needed to be challenged by the next level of hockey. At the end of his junior year at Dartmouth, Matt was ready to move on again and signed a contract with the Boston Bruins. We did right by Matt and his journey continues.

In the end, I know I served Matt's best interests. Herbie at some level had an influence in Matt's career ascent. As a leader, Herbie showed me how to lead, how to look out for the best interests of those counting on and trusting in us leaders to lead them. I hope and suspect that sometime in the future, Matt Lindblad will be doing the same for another young life that places his trust in him to lead him down the best path. When you see leadership, it sticks with you and gets passed along. I hope Matt passes it along as well and I suspect he will.

Years later, however things happen, I felt like I was really getting to know Herbie fairly well. I saw him on occasion at a local garden center in White Bear Lake. He liked his gardening or plants, whatever exactly it was, I cannot remember as we often talked hockey or a bit of politics. He told me he was a mix of Republican and Libertarian. I know he believed in the faith and power within the individual. I would have loved to see him try politics. He would have made everyone mad at some point, but no doubt he would have challenged conventional thinking and the status quo!

At that time, I was getting the itch to get back into coaching on more of a full-time basis. I shared this with Herb and he was at the ready again to help in any way he could. In the months before his death, when the phone would ring and often after 10pm with our kids already in bed, my wife MaryBeth and I knew it was Herb. MaryBeth might answer the phone and then summon me by calling out, "It's your new best friend." It wasn't that we were new best friends, it was just that we had something in common; we both cared about kids and the game of hockey. And in that regard, Herb and I talked about a number of ideas on how to improve the game and maybe how I could get back and more involved in hockey (at the time I was out of coaching full time though working with my kids in sports like many fathers do). Knowing Herb was knowing he was never too happy about much of anything. He always saw a problem that needed to be fixed if just the right people got involved or quit putting politics in front of progress. The status quo was no friend of Herbie's. I could go on and on, but anybody who knew Herb, knew he had little time for politicking when the solution seemed at least to him, to be pretty straightforward.

He said what he thought, honestly to everyone, all the time. He and my dad were surprisingly alike. They challenged friend and foe alike on their views and actions. Not the kind of behavior that plays well in our all too often superficial, be careful with every word political environment of today. Leaders often make enemies of sorts. Their ability to see and willingness to take new paths are often a threat to those who make a living or are comfortable with the old way of doing things. Herbie in particular had a way of making those comfortable in the old way of doing things not so comfortable. It was one of his secrets to success…no one ever got comfortable! He was always challenging conventional wisdom and the status quo.

I don't know if I have met a stronger leader in the world of hockey. He understood dissent, that dissent is not a negative to an organization or a system, but a positive to its continued development. Heck, our country is founded in large part on positive dissent. Dissent is simply a challenge, a challenge to existing ideas and existing direction.

Countries need their citizens and leaders to dissent. Relationships of all kinds need dissent. Corporations need it. Whatever track any of these entities is on today might be a great track, but not forever. Change is inevitable and necessary. Herb knew this as well as anyone and was unafraid to voice his dissent with the current way of things. The thing with leaders like Herbie is that they inherently know that dissent is often not popular. There are always those invested on the current track, the current ways of doing things. Herb knew who he was and what he stood for and was willing to stand up for what he thought was right, or maybe a new path worth considering. Stubborn maybe, but Herbie was always strong in his convictions and unafraid to challenge current ideas and structures. He didn't go status quo when selected to coach the 1980 Olympic team, and we all know how great that story ends.

If you saw the movie *Miracle*, there is a short bit early in the movie where he simply infers the team is already picked. The hierarchy of the governing body of USA Hockey would provide Herbie a selection committee for the team, or at minimum a "sounding board" of feedback for the coaches on player selection. Well, Herbie had different ideas. He knew it wasn't just the best and most purely talented players who win championships; it was a mix of players who can mix into particular roles. Herbie I think knew that if left to the powers of a selection committee, there would be great haggling over kids who have great talent and shouldn't be left off the team for a kid with less "pure" talent. He knew what he wanted for this team and he knew he needed certain roles players. Indeed, he selected a great blend of players, many of who played in the NHL, but also a handful of players who never did, and yet filled their roles on the team with great passion though with arguably less pure talent. He did it his way, a way in which his many years of training had suggested to him was a winning formula.

I once took on the challenge of getting Herbie to agree to become part of an auction for the Midwest High School Elite League. The High School Elite League was a fall league for the better players in Minnesota/Wisconsin and the Dakotas to supplement what can be a short high school hockey season. This league was started by another leader in John Russo. John has long advocated for better coaching and nurturing of our young players. The High School Elite League played right into his mission of providing better opportunities for others. John Russo works selflessly for the sake of others. The league was always in need of help on the funding side.

The idea John and I came up with was to have a season long "auction" at the various game sites. Folks could bid on certain packages, all for the financial benefit of Elite League operations. I came up with the idea of having Herbie be an auction item. The winning bid could have him come to speak at a corporate outing, or to a bunch of young people, maybe a group of hockey players or maybe a group of future leaders from any walk of life. It wouldn't cost anyone anything and we would probably raise a good chunk of money.

When I first called Herbie with the idea, he was his usual pain-in-the-rear-end self. He shared with me everything he thought the Elite League needed to do to improve itself. After an hour of hearing him out, I simply told Herbie in a somewhat exasperated tone that all faults aside, there wasn't going to be an Elite League if we couldn't find creative ways to fund the league. He almost immediately became the soft and caring Herbie that existed underneath all the tough exterior and told me that when he went up north to the Hall of Fame Golf Tournament, he would be sure to help get people interested in raising funds for the league. As that weekend unfolded, he left me a message on my voice mail as to his progress. On his way home Herbie died in a car accident. I still had his phone message on my phone's voice mail. I kept the message for a day or so after Herbie's death, not sure if I owed it to myself or others to not erase one of his last communications. It felt kind of morbid to keep it on my phone so I erased it. Bottom line is Herbie was THE guy to get such funds raised. He was our hockey leader, maybe not just in Minnesota, but nation-wide. He was THE guy to get a lot of things done. These many years later, we still have not found THE leader to fill the void left by his passing.

I have often thought about what great leaders my dad and Herb were. Herb may have been different from my dad in some ways, but the two had a lot in common also. The world is a better place having had those two in it. Neither minced their words. You got an honest and educated answer when you asked either of them a question. They both knew their trades extremely well and while aware of the politics that surrounded their trades, neither were deterred from saying and doing what they believed to be right. I also suspect, for both, their word was their bond. If they shook your hand and looked you in the eye and said you had a deal, you had a deal that didn't need to be written on paper. They were men of honor. They were men of integrity and they spoke unafraid of others' judgments. They spoke most often on their vision to make the world better for others, not for themselves. It is a value our great country and leaders of many industries need to return to. And maybe most importantly, both really cared about the people and things entrusted to them. They were stewards of the world they lived in. Their industry, their families would benefit from their voice. They wanted those around them to flourish and succeed and they wanted all to do it with integrity. No action taken by either of these men lacked in integrity!

MORE LESSONS...

I am not sure why, but in today's world, if words are spoken that are seen as somehow controversial or challenging the politically correct or conventional wisdom, we seem too often as a society to castigate, be intolerant, shun or even litigate. I suspect it has always been that way but in today's world, the words of any leader travel fast. We as a society need to embrace dissent; listen to it and see if there is a new direction worth taking. We especially need to do so when the words are unpopular.

We also need to be aware of, to recognize those voices with a vested interest in keeping things the same as they may not want the new path, they just want their path. Maybe they are simply ignorant. Maybe their path is lined with their own benefits, sometimes financial, sometimes emotional. Sometimes their resistance stems from a lack in their own ability to acknowledge a path smarter or better than the one they themselves helped to construct. It can be hard on their ego. It also takes a leader to acknowledge others' positive dissent and a better vision for a better direction and not as an attack on "their" vision but simply a better path. And a leader will follow a better path, often putting his or her own personal knowledge to play to make this new path even better.

Truly good leaders will embrace dissent. Dissent is just an opposing view. Leaders understand and appreciate an opposing view. Opposing views against the current tide is how any individual or organization makes course corrections. Great leaders listen and then make decisions based not on their own egos, but what is best for the team, or corporation, or country. When you hear a politician acknowledge the positive dissent of an opposing view and then argue the points of contention on the merits of the idea…well, then you have a leader and not a politician. In my opinion we don't have enough of these types of people in political offices today.

Leaders surround themselves with the talent of other leaders. Blind and ignorant changes of direction are just that. Leaders want continued education; they listen to the smart people around them and are not afraid of dissent. They recognize dissent as a healthy part of a process of finding new and better. Leaders lead and leaders are also courageous enough to follow the rightful path blazed by others.

If you get a chance, go to YouTube and check out the Starlings Over Ottmoor. This is a YouTube video of birds that flock in the evenings to protect one another from predators. Thousands of these birds gather to fly together in the early evening. Their flight, their dance is a constantly changing, ever-evolving movement that appears something closer to poetry or artistic dance than to anything one would think a group of birds could create. But in their effort to protect the group I see much more than artistic movement. I see a group of alternating leaders who are unafraid to dissent, willing to not follow the flock in a straight line influenced only by the direction of the group. Many eyes, many leaders both create and follow new directions that are beneficial to the group's safety. It is a thing of beauty and worth a few minutes to watch one of nature's many marvels…and if birds can lead each other in harmony, so can we people!

CHAPTER 5:
PIONEERS AND LEADERS:
CHALLENGING THE STATUS QUO

What often happens within each of our mind-sets when things seem to be going perfectly well? In my experience, it seems too often individuals and teams get complacent. *Fat and happy* is a phrase we sometimes use to describe the feelings and mind-set we develop when good times abound. The good times will last forever, right? We all know that is not true. So why at times do we get complacent and not search even harder for a better path, especially when things are going well? I think we all know things are always changing and evolving. Whatever we are today, whatever direction we are headed, there is a better version and route just around the corner if we keep looking.

Leaders and pioneers quite often challenge conventional wisdom for this very reason. When things seem perfectly fine, leaders know a new challenge is just over the horizon. People who lead are always looking beyond their current horizon to find the next best way of things.

Hockey in Minnesota, for example, seemed perfectly fine to many in the Minnesota hockey community long before the advent of Junior Hockey. We had a great college culture both at the Division I level, as well as the Division II/III level. We had more than our share of players moving from the high school ranks on to the various college programs. Overall, we had a great system in place for many, but not a great system for everybody.

Minnesota hockey was not in relative terms to its production of college players, producing a great number of professionals.

That was still Canada's domain. We here in Minnesota were impressed with the results we had, including the development of one of the great high school tournaments of any kind in America—the Minnesota State High School Hockey Tournament. This tournament, then and now, sells out an NHL size venue. Hockey in Minnesota was perfectly fine….maybe, however, the hockey community was also a bit fat and happy!

RON WOODEY: HOCKEY PIONEER

Hockey pioneer Ron Woodey came to the scene of this perfectly content hockey community in the late 1960s. If there was a single Grand-Daddy or maybe I should call him the PIONEER/LEADER/INNOVATOR of Junior Hockey in America, in my opinion it is the late Ron Woodey. Before my playing in the World Junior Tournament and all the college recruiting that came into my life, I came to know Ron Woodey as the General Manager and founder of the St. Paul Vulcans. During my time as a Vulcan player, I didn't get to know Ron all that well as we had a strong coach in Doug Woog. Doug was our communication man. That said, we all knew Ron was one tough old fella.

I still don't know much about Ron's younger life. Like many Minnesota youngsters, he played hockey in his youth. Eventually Ron became an entrepreneur. He bought a Dairy Queen I was told. I don't know how he came to so strongly believe that Junior Hockey was a missing link in the Minnesota and American development model, but he did. By the time most of us had come to know Ron, he was not just the General Manager of the St. Paul Vulcans but he was also a scout for the Philadelphia Flyers. He took great pride in the relationship he had with the Flyer organization.

Each year Ron gathered the players and coaches to begin the season with an introductory talk about what it meant to play for the St. Paul Vulcans. To this day I wish I had the foresight to video record it.

Ron told us all, new players and old, new coaches and old, how things had to be and what the St. Paul Vulcans would stand for. He told us that our organization would be one that the others wanted to emulate. He also let us know in no uncertain terms that we would be the team in the league that all the other teams would not look forward to playing. We would become such a team he would say: *Not because we will be dirty or chippy, but because we will be the team that requires the highest level of sacrifice to play and beat.* He wanted every foot of ice to be contested. Over and over, Ron also always told us: *Each foot of ice will have to be earned by our opponents.* The word he loved to use was *miserable,* as in playing the Vulcans should be and needed to be a *miserable* experience for our opponents. It was an inspiring talk, one I listened to year after year even in my coaching days with equal enthusiasm. Ron set the level of expectation for all of us each year.

Ron, more than most, saw the need for Junior Hockey to develop in the United States. In a sport where other countries allowed their players to develop to the age of 20, our United States and Minnesota high-school system was leaving too many 18-year-olds behind with no place to go and develop in these very formidable years of 18 to 20. I was certainly one of those players. I entered Junior Hockey a slight 160-pound 18-year-old and left junior hockey a 184-pound 20-year-old ready for major college hockey. Without Junior Hockey and the St. Paul Vulcans, I would never have realized my goal of playing major college hockey. I have Ron Woodey to thank.

Minnesota as a state was arguably the best hockey talent provider for the higher levels of hockey in the United States, particularly Division-I college hockey. That is what made Ron's vision so incredible at the time. Why would anyone want to dissent from the status quo or innovate in a state when things were seemingly going so well? That is what leaders and pioneers do, they innovate. They make better. They do not sit status quo; they constantly seek new ideas for new directions.

Minnesota did then and still does a lot of good things for the development of its hockey-playing culture. Ron Woodey and the advent of Junior Hockey have made the Minnesota hockey culture even better! But it is not just Minnesota hockey that has Ron to thank. The Midwest Junior League grew into the USHL—the premier junior league in America. Over 1/3 of all

Division I college players come thru the USHL. Then on top of that, over 30% of all NHL players in today's game come from the college ranks...that is progress!

Many years after Ron's innovations in Junior Hockey, when the 2013 Hobey Baker top ten finalists were announced, acknowledging the ten best college hockey players in the country, Minnesota led the way with four finalists...all of whom played Junior Hockey in the USHL. When the hat-trick finalists (the three finalists for the Hobey Baker) were announced, all three had played in the USHL, the Junior League that Ron Woodey was most responsible for. While it is likely none of the finalists know anything of Ron Woodey, they have him to thank at least in part for their success.

It is interesting to look back at some of the mind-sets of the hockey community back before the advent of Junior Hockey in the US, before Junior Hockey in the United States really took hold. Many within the hockey culture, especially in Minnesota, often talked as if it was cheating that successful teams like the University of North Dakota and Michigan Tech University were even taken seriously. *Seriously* might not be the right word; maybe the right word is *purely*. Teams like North Dakota had older players, many had played...Junior Hockey. It was like they were cheating! This mind-set was one born of ignorance. The Minnesota hockey community didn't know what it didn't know. It was they and their system of high school hockey that was not the norm throughout the world of hockey.

The Minnesota hockey community viewed itself then and maybe it still does today as somehow more pure. The Minnesota "pure" culture loves to promote skating, passing, offense, and academics. As Minnesotans viewed it back then, kids played high school sports and then they went to college. They went directly to college! Colleges like North Dakota and Michigan Tech were playing with a stacked deck with players who had played Junior Hockey and then advanced to the college ranks often as 20-year-old freshman and eventually 24-year-old-seniors.

What Minnesotans didn't understand back then is it was *they* who really didn't fit in with the rest of the world. It was *they* and a couple of other states, most notably Massachusetts, who played mainly high school hockey. That was not true of the rest of the world. Ron Woodey understood that. Hockey was and is a "world" sport. There were and are great players in the game from many countries and virtually all have played junior hockey. High school hockey was as odd to those in these foreign countries as Junior Hockey was to Minnesota. Ron Woodey simply wanted to bring a new vision and opportunity for many to our hockey community through the development of Junior Hockey programs. He succeeded.

Back in those days the United States was not on par with Canada, nor Russia or Czechoslovakia. More importantly to guys like Ron, many young people, especially in Ron's home state of Minnesota, were not being afforded the same opportunities to develop through those huge physical and emotional developmental years of 18-20. Ron rightly concluded that the United States needed junior programs also. He saw what was needed; he innovated even in the face of a culture that thought it had developed the system as it ought to be. Ron went against much conventional wisdom.

For many years, Ron remained the voice and face of Junior Hockey in America. The league expanded. Franchises came and went. Ron remained. His work and dedication never wavered. That said, with all Ron did and all his extra hard work, those within our organization knew they should never forget his words, his direction for the franchise. We were all part of his stated vision—to each do our part to make each game a *miserable* experience for our opponents. No one believed in toughness like Ron Woodey.

If you know hockey you know that back in those days, back in the 1970s, Ron's other team, the Philadelphia Flyers, were also called the *Broadstreet Bullies*. The Flyers were real-life bullies. Ron was proud of his NHL team, and more often than not, he wore his black leather Flyers jacket around our locker room. He was proud of how tough the Flyers were and very proud that he was instrumental in their selection of St. Paul native and former St. Paul Vulcan Paul Holmgren. Holmgren scored buckets of goals for the Flyers, but he was probably more well known for dropping the mitts and physical play. Paul Holmgren is to this day the GM of the Flyers; a fact I think Ron would still be quite proud of were he still alive.

One thing I always believed about Ron as a scout is that if he said a player *could play*, the player *could play*! There would be nothing gentle in his description. Ron didn't like soft. In hockey no player wants to be called soft. Honest is good. Tough is good. Soft is not so good. I suspect Ron thought I was soft at the beginning of my junior career. Looking back, I am sure I was soft. But Junior Hockey works that out of you. I was very proud upon arrival for my second year with the Vulcans when Mr. Woodey (as all us players called him out of respect) handed me the jersey with the captain's "C" on the shoulder. Those are things a leader relishes. I must have come a long ways in his eyes for sure.

In my opinion, the 1976 St. Paul Vulcans were one of the greatest Junior Teams of all time. It included NHL great and current Philadelphia General Manager Paul Holmgren and a bunch of not only good players, but tough, tough, tough players. Vulcan games at Wakota Arena in South St. Paul against the very tough and rugged Thunder Bay team, with Olge Gordthorp, gave the franchise a new image. It was an image of tough. It was an image like that of the Broadstreet Bullies. It was the image Ron strived for—a tough and miserable team to play against.

The Vulcan's Sunday night games were played as part of a third leg of Thunder Bay's trip home after a weekend series elsewhere. It drew sell-out crowds, not necessarily to watch the hockey, but to watch the heavyweight fights. The Vulcans, with Holmgren, Les Auge, Craig Hamner, Jim Boo and Jim Cunningham, had more than enough players who could drop the mitts. Jim Cunningham, from Mounds View and at just 180 pounds may have been the Vulcan's best fighter of the group. While the team's toughness was often on display in these games, make no mistake, this team put Junior Hockey in the United States on the map with its great play. This team played four games in '76 against major junior teams in Canada, and won them all. This Vulcan team was allowed in Canada's Centennial Cup, which in that era was the Tier 2 National Championship (today I believe it is called the RBC Cup). The Vulcans went all the way to the Centennial Cup finals in '76...the last time a U.S. team was ever allowed in the tournament. One does not have to wonder why no US team was ever invited back!

The majority of this great Vulcan team moved on to play Division I college hockey and another good handful progressed to the professional ranks. In my early years of coaching the Vulcans, I would stop in to visit with a high school coach after a high school game and shared my vision and desire to recruit one of his key players. I was often told by this coach (in essence): *Oh, I know that team—bunch of fighters they are...You don't want my player—he's too smart for that league; he is going to college after high school.* They didn't say it quite that way, but that is what they were saying.

This Junior Hockey thing didn't fit into the Minnesota hockey community's self-constructed box of *pure hockey*. I had to work hard to change their perceptions. That 1976 team, as good as it was, had carried a reputation that many in the Minnesota hockey community didn't identify with. For what seemed the longest of times, this reputation wouldn't go away. Junior Hockey was *goon* hockey, or so they thought...

When you think back, Ron's development of the Vulcans and the merger with the USHL to become America's only Tier 1 Junior League was simply positive dissent from the status quo. It was essentially a leader's change of direction. There wasn't any Junior Hockey in the Minnesota area. Only a leader could see a different vision and see why it was needed and what its purpose would be. For many, the high school system in Minnesota was *the* right track! Why would anyone want to dissent from the successful status quo? Plenty of young people were going to colleges out of the state, and if one wasn't ready for D-I at age 18, then there was nothing wrong with going D-III. Or so the status quo maintained. Ron knew that formula wasn't serving everyone.

An important lesson to any aspiring leader or pioneer is that with any change, there are folks with a vested interest in the status quo. The people with the most interest vested in the status quo are exactly the people who will be the most opposed to much of what is being introduced by the new leader and pioneer. Many people in Minnesota didn't care for the advent of Junior Hockey. They saw it as a threat to *their* way. In the backs of their minds, they wondered what might happen should Junior Hockey get popular in Minnesota, like it was in Canada. *What might happen to our high school system?* This was the concern of many who had a vested interest in our long-standing tradition of the high school system in Minnesota.

Some of these concerns were valid. In Canada, kids were dropping out of school to pursue hockey, not a value shared by an education-conscious community like Minnesota. Still, there was a fear—if this Junior Hockey system became popular, this new way of things might entice a high school player to opt for Junior Hockey instead of high school hockey. For those invested in the status quo this would not be a good thing. It could, in their view, affect the quality of the high school game that many had spent years trying to build. It might even affect their jobs. These voices were heard loud and clear. This debate still plays out today, especially in the states of Minnesota and Massachusetts.

Some in these education-conscious communities could not support Junior Hockey even in cases like mine. Their idea of the *right* track was right from high school to college. If you weren't good enough coming out of high school, then why waste your valuable time? Their thinking was get on to college and get on with your life. I think that particular thinking has changed as Junior Hockey is certainly more widely accepted, but there is still friction there between what has been and what is now.

I will never forget my high school graduation party. I am sure my mother bragged quite a bit about my very good high school grades along with some of the recruiting letters I had been receiving for baseball and hockey. I was likely to be the first in my immediate family to attend a four-year college. So at my graduation party, when friends and relatives excitedly asked me where I was heading off to college and I replied with *I'm not going straight to college, I am going to play Junior Hockey*, I saw looks of disbelief. I know I saw looks of friends and family who thought I must be hanging out with the wrong inner-city St. Paul crowd doing drugs on the street corner. Certainly I must be destined to achieve much less than my potential.

Because of Ron Woodey's leadership and development of this new Junior Hockey direction, I was able to also take my own alternative track. I turned down my baseball future and pursued my passion. I took that alternative path, which at that point in my life was my first really good decision. Because of the Vulcans, I was afforded the opportunity to develop and play in the World Junior Tournament. I was able to enjoy a four-year career at the University of Minnesota where we won a National Championship. My junior year may have been the most fun of all. We were the best team in the nation, but finished second when Wisconsin upset us in the NCAA final game. I was fortunate in playing on the leading scoring line in America, a line with two All-Americans on it (Steve Ulseth and Neal Broten). Who could not be grateful?

CHANGING COURSE

After my four-year career at the University of Minnesota, serving as Captain my senior year, I was off to my next chapter. In 1982, I attended New York Rangers training camp in Rye, NY. I made it through a couple of cuts, but did not make the final cut. No worries, I thought, as my goal was to play for the U.S. National Team. Back then, they would put a National Team together the year preceding the Olympics as part of Olympic preparation. After getting a taste of international competition with the Junior National Team, I couldn't think of anything more appealing than playing in the 1984 Olympics. Well, I also got cut later on from the U.S. National Team. I think all of us cut from that last team think the team made a mistake and I have always thought that the National Team made a mistake cutting me, but maybe it was a blessing in disguise.

As I was contemplating playing in the minor pros or getting into coaching, I went back to St. Paul and visited Ron Woodey. At the time, the St. Paul Vulcans were really struggling both on the ice and off. I recall going to a game and they barely had half a roster dressed for their game. Very few people were in the stands. I volunteered to help at a couple of practices and really felt the team lacked leadership. The team had reached a low point in popularity. The players didn't seem as dedicated. The team was falling behind their USHL contemporaries. Their contemporaries drew a good number of spectators thus it generated good revenues. The other USHL teams were able to not only pay the bills, but pay good coaches and recruiters. The Vulcans could no longer compete favorably. I felt I needed to help.

The organization meant too much to me to be happy about what I was seeing. I let Ron know that I was quite interested in getting into coaching, and coaching the Vulcans was a goal and even a duty in my mind. Ron said he had always thought I would make a great coach and said we would talk more as the season progressed. He gave me a strong indication that there could be a coaching change at the end of the year and I would be a strong consideration for the job if that were to happen. It was decision time for me: keep playing minor pro or go back to school and finish the three classes I still needed to graduate. I was confident the Vulcans would make a coaching change and even that I would be that next coach. So I decided to sign up for classes at the University of Minnesota and be prepared the following year to go into coaching full time. I was about to meet another series of outstanding leaders and pioneers—a group of truly world-class leaders and innovators that again influenced my life in very positive ways.

MIRACLE ON ICE...THE SPENGLER CUP...REAL WORLD PIONEERS

Some of us are old enough to have experienced the *Miracle* of the 1980 United States Olympic Hockey team. Others may have experienced the Gold Medal-Winning 1980 Olympic team via the movie *Miracle*. The movie depicts the triumph of the 1980 United States Olympic Hockey team led by Herb

Brooks. You may recall that half the team consisted of former U of Minnesota Golden Gophers players. I was a sophomore at the U of Minnesota at the time of the 1980 Olympic triumph.

At the time of the 1980 Miracle on Ice, I was a sophomore at the U of Minnesota. Unbeknownst to me and most others, at this very time two people with direct ties to the University of Minnesota were actively promoting the University of Minnesota college hockey team to be the first ever college team invited to Davos, Switzerland, to participate in the very prestigious European tournament, the Spengler Cup. These US and University of Minnesota college kids winning Olympic Gold in 1980 were just what our promoters needed to get us invited to the Spengler Cup a couple of years later.

The Spengler Cup was and still is a major hockey tournament played each year in Davos, Switzerland. The Spengler Cup is kind of like the European hockey version of what Wimbledon is to tennis. Top professional teams from around the world are invited to Davos to play in this Christmastime tournament. Back in the day, Russia and Czechoslovakia were communist countries that did not allow their top players to defect to the west for the big money of the NHL. The teams they sent to the Spengler Cup were the caliber of our top NHL teams. It was like the U.S. sending the Pittsburg Penguins and Canada sending the Montreal Canadians. Our NHL teams were in the midst of their season and the league would not allow any of their teams to attend. We had no like caliber teams to send to the tournament.

There was still a long-standing desire of the tournament organizers to attract teams from Canada and/or the United States. There was a small current of thought led by German immigrant and U of Minnesota team doctor, Dr. George Nagobads, that if you want a representative from the United States, that consideration should be given for a top college team like the University of Minnesota. Dr. Nagobads, a wonderful man, smallish in stature with a thick German accent, had relationships in Europe and had been promoting for several years the idea of a U.S. college team like ours at the U of Minnesota for consideration in the Spengler Cup.

The rest of the world did not understand high school and college hockey. They knew a different development model. The prevailing thought in Davos remained that a college team like Minnesota could not compete on this world stage with these high-quality, world-class teams. So year after year, in spite of the urging by Dr. Nagobads, and eventually former U of Minnesota alumnus and 1972 Olympian Craig Sarner (who eventually coached the host Davos team), the idea of a college team from the United States continued to gain little traction.

Then the U.S. Olympic team did the unthinkable and won the 1980 Gold Medal against the very best players that Russia and Czechoslovakia and most of the rest of the world had to offer. The U.S. didn't just beat a great team, they beat a team of all-stars; the best of the best from these countries. The 1980 Olympic victory was the advertising Dr. Nagobads and Coach Sarner needed to strengthen their argument. Not only was the 1980 team comprised entirely of players from the NCAA, but 11 members of the team were from the U of Minnesota. Once the Davos committee saw how talented these college kids were, and that most of the team came from the same college…the invitation Dr. Nagobads and Craig Sarner had lobbied for was finally extended. I was the captain of the Gopher team in 1981-82, the year the University of Minnesota attended this prestigious tournament.

Before we left for Davos, we were given a lecture on beating jet lag, a new experience for most of us. When you travel through seven time zones, your internal body clock gets pretty goofed up. Traveling this far is always a challenge. The plane ride was about six hours. We then boarded busses—one bus for the team, the other bus for a slew of parents and supporters as well as some local media who came along to witness and record the event. The bus ride was another several hours. It was going to be a grueling trip but rewarded with a once in-a-lifetime groundbreaking experience to serve as ambassadors of our university and our country.

Amid all the travel frenzy, little did I know that one of the media personnel was in charge of following the team to document this historic event. He was a young man by the name of Stanley E. Hubbard. Young Stan, as we called him, came from one of the truly pioneering media families in America. Our paths were about to cross more than once.

At the time of the Spengler Cup trip, Young Stan was a college student at the University of Minnesota. His dad Stanley S. Hubbard and his grandfather Stanley E. Hubbard were broadcast pioneers. Their most visible properties to us in Minnesota were and still are, KSTP-TV-ABC as well as radio stations KSTP-AM1500 and KS-95 FM. Today Young Stan is the developer and CEO of REELZ TV Network, just another of many accomplishments of he and his family.

The Hubbard family was the first privately held company to put a satellite in space. Though there were great ways to deliver television programming, including a new technology we call cable TV, they saw an even better way to deliver programming. They developed a system via satellite of program delivery that could serve more people and more locations. It was revolutionary. They eventually sold their interest in this start-up enterprise in what we now know as Direct-TV. Their list of accomplishments is long and distinguished.

Still a college student himself, Young Stan was along on the trip to Davos to play helper and film runner for his KSTP-TV news crew that came along to cover this historic trip. I suspect Stan's parents thought it would be a good education to travel to central Europe and help their news crew. I recall Young Stan helping with lighting for interviews and the like. I saw him out and about, but we didn't get to know each other much. Stan was working, and I, as a captain of my hockey team, was there to play hockey. More about Young Stan in a bit...

Our Gopher hockey team played well overall in the Spengler Cup but didn't win a game. We lost game one 5-4 to the Czechoslovakia team. The locals knew we were the underdogs and everyone loves an underdog. They seemingly fell in love with us right away. I think they loved our speed and enthusiasm and our ability to keep up with teams with superior talent. I think they also liked that we played more physical. That means we initiated more body checks, a trait especially back then of teams from North America, but not so much of Europe.

We initiated physical contact early and often against the Czechs. The fans cheered right to the final buzzer. We then lost a close game to a team from West Germany. We were told the Davos crowd particularly didn't like the Germans back then. When we gave the German team all they could handle, staying physical and standing up to them, the fans seemed to fall in love with us even more. I recall an altercation in front of our bench. It wasn't really a fight, but let's just say we weren't going to be bullied by the team from Germany, and this won us great favor with our new supporters from Davos.

Game three was against the host team Davos in one of the more unique games I have ever participated in. They were coached by former Gopher Craig Sarner. The home crowd of Davos cheered for both teams equally, which was pretty cool. We lost that game 5-2 but I really captured a feeling that I will never forget. It was a feeling that most games should be like that one, where the fans appreciate the talents of both teams. For a loss, it was a very cool experience.

The final game was against Spartek Moscow, one of the premier teams from the Soviet Union. They were the equivalent of a top NHL team. They beat us 9-1, and probably if they had really tried, could have nearly doubled the score. Poor Paul Ostby, our very good goalie and eventual team MVP, was left to fend for himself way too often. We would have needed to play about 8 players to protect him against this superior opponent. We were out of our league in that game and just didn't have the ability to support our goaltender. It was a great experience however, one none of us will ever forget. While we didn't win a game, we represented our university, college hockey and our country very well.

It was less than a year later when I was cut from the U.S. National team. As I said earlier, I talked with Ron Woodey, decided I would go back to school, and hoped to be the next Vulcan coach. I knew my old team, the St. Paul Vulcans, were at an all-time low and in need of new leadership.

What I didn't know is that Ron Woodey had gone to Hubbard Broadcasting and had spoken with broadcast industry pioneer Stanley S. Hubbard (Young Stan's dad) to ask for help. Mr. Hubbard, as I still call him, was an ex-Gopher hockey player himself, though he says he didn't play very much. Mostly he said that he watched the greatest player in the history of Minnesota hockey play. The player he was referring to was John Mayasich, a native of Eveleth, Minnesota. John holds all the scoring records in Minnesota high school hockey history as well as all the scoring records at the University of Minnesota. He is without question one of the finest people I have ever met. I also didn't realize at the time there were some stars aligning as John Mayasich was also the President of Hubbard Radio. I had met John the previous two years at the University of Minnesota annual Gopher awards banquet.

As a testament to how good John Mayasich was as a player, I will share a little Hobey Baker Award ceremony moment. I attended the 1986 Hobey Baker Award Ceremony at the Decathlon Club in Minneapolis, where Bill Cleary, the Head Coach of the Harvard Crimson, was about to introduce the winner of the 1986 Hobey Baker Award, to his own player Scott Fusco. In his address, he first greeted the many people in attendance at the Minneapolis Decathlon Club. Coach Cleary talked about what a great opportunity it was for him to again meet up with his many hockey acquaintances. He pointed to our table; sitting across from me was John. He said how particularly great it was to see his old friend and Olympic teammate John Mayasich again. He said something to the effect of: *...And let me tell you how good John Mayasich was. Back in our day, I believe that had we had a Hobey Baker Award, that John Mayasich would have won the award four straight years!* That's Mr. Cleary saying that, not me. I do know that John totally blushed from the incredible compliment. He was and is as humble as they come.

The whole Hubbard family seemed to be hockey enthusiasts. All the Hubbard boys played and appreciated the work and sacrifice it took to be successful in the sport. Young Stan had actually played for the Vulcans a couple of years after my playing days with the Vulcans. That is how Mr. Woodey knew the Hubbards so well. Ron and the Vulcans needed help. Ron approached Mr. Hubbard to ask if they would consider buying and financing an organization that did so much good for so many local aspiring hockey players. The current group could no longer afford to operate the team in this growing league. Before I knew any of this and just before I was going to go back to the university and sign up for classes, I read in the newspaper that Hubbard Broadcasting bought the St. Paul Vulcans. This was just weeks after my conversation with Mr. Woodey and just a day or two before I was going to head back to school.

I remember being devastated. I had said *no* to a couple of minor-pro teams that had called to have me come play for them. I did so because of what now appeared to be my foolish confidence of getting the next head coaching job with the Vulcans. I guess when you are as young as I was, you don't always consider all the factors. Now the whole idea of me being the next Vulcan coach looked a lot less likely of becoming a reality.

As fate would have it, I continued with the plan and headed off to the University of Minnesota and got in the registration line to sign up for winter classes. The lines were organized alphabetically. Being a Hartzell, I got into the "H" line and guess who I turn around to see just behind me also in the "H" line? As fate would have it, it was none other than Young Stan Hubbard. When the stars align, they really align!

I allowed fate to hold my hand I guess. I turned around and I asked Young Stan if he remembered me from the trip to Davos and the Spengler Cup. He said that he did and our conversation began. I asked him about the very recent news of their family buying the Vulcan team and he told me how excited they were to buy the team. It was a team he played for just a couple of years previous.

He told me that they had a bunch of ideas on how to upgrade the franchise and lead the USHL in the pursuit of a stronger and better league. He told me that indeed they planned to hire a new coach and gave me some big-name ex-NHL players as potential candidates. I was disappointed at not making his initial short list. I basically told him that while I appreciated his excitement, I was pretty much depressed and gave him my short story as to why I was there in that line that day. A big part of my being there of course was the anticipation of being the next Vulcan coach.

Young Stan told me weeks later that when he asked me that day why I wanted to coach the team, that he was taken aback by my simple answer which was something to the effect of *because it is just something I want and need to do*. He could tell by my answer that I was certain that somehow it was my destiny. Leaders see things differently. They recognize things others do not. More than anything he recognized my motivation. My *why*, my motivation, came from the heart. In psychology they call that intrinsic motivation—the kind that is deeply internal and personal. That is always powerful motivation and it made an impression on Young Stan that day. What happened next is a life lesson for us all.

IT REALLY DOES TAKES ONE TO KNOW ONE

I eventually came to understand that this young man, Stanley E. Hubbard, was a leader, a very good leader in development in his own right. He has led companies that have become huge successes like Direct-TV and today, REELZ TV. I believe to this day that Young Stan is the best combination of good human being and smart businessman I have ever met. Stan liked my answer that day in the "H" line, my firm belief in my own destiny. He recognized my motivation came from within. My *why* permeated my very being. He gave me his business card that day in the "H" line at the University of Minnesota and invited me to come and see him. I called and made an appointment to go and see him to discuss the job a few days later.

There was a lot I didn't know at the time. I didn't know that Young Stan's father, Mr. Hubbard, was entrusting him to run this hockey franchise as one of his first full-fledged business enterprises. In the end, he was going to be the decision maker. I also didn't know that this young man was wise beyond his years. He had been attending meetings with his dad and family for years. His talk around the dinner table often had to do with business, with the nurturing of leadership and innovation. The Hubbard family members were then and continue to be incredibly successful leaders and pioneers. Young Stan grew up in this environment.

The family understood more than most about leadership. They understood doubters, those that didn't want to embrace positive dissent and innovation. They took calculated risk for things they believed in. They created things that previously didn't exist. They had doubters each step of the way. I would come to find the entire family nothing short of amazing. And like all the great leaders I have known, their belief system was based on values. Their most important and stated values were honesty and integrity. I was walking into something both profound and unique.

I also didn't know that John Mayasich, the all-time U of Minnesota hockey great, who I had only at that point met in a couple of brief moments, would be instrumental in the decision-making process as well. Above all, I didn't yet know how much a leader recognizes and appreciates another leader.

I showed up for that first meeting at Hubbard Broadcasting on University Avenue in St. Paul. I was escorted to the third floor to the company's executive's office. I walk into Young Stan's office for that initial meeting and was welcomed to sit down. Here is how the important first part of the conversation went to the best of my recollection.

Young Stan: *Do you know why I have invited you here today?*

Me: *Yes, I sure do. I am here to talk with you about being the next coach of the St. Paul Vulcans.*

Young Stan: *No, that's not it. Do you know why I (and I heard the emphasis on "why I")...Do you know **why I** have invited you to come talk with me today?*

Me (as I was allowing his words and motivations to sink in): *Maybe not. Why have you invited me here today?*

Young Stan: *You remember we met a year ago over at the Spengler Cup in Davos.*

Me: *Of course I remember that.*

Young Stan: *You remember the long first day of travel?*

Me: *For sure I do.*

Young Stan: *Well, you know how long a day it was, hours of travel, first by air, then by bus, and we were told how to beat jet lag and all that. Me, I was watching you. Not sure why, but I was watching you closely. After the long flight I was on the same bus as the team and I was thinking to myself, there's the captain of the Gophers. What's he all about? Will he be chasing girls? Is he a drinker? I am not sure why, but I was wondering if maybe you didn't have all the best of intentions. Maybe you were here in Europe and about to chase the college lifestyle of girls and drinking and so on.*

At this point I really didn't know where he was going with this, then this wise-beyond-his-years young man finished with:

Young Stan: *Then at the end of that very long day of travel, we were all tired. Two busloads of hockey team and supporters with all their gear pull up in front of the hotel and you were the first person off the bus and immediately began unpacking the bus. I kept watching you and when everyone else quit because they thought the job was done, or tired or lazy, you were still the one guy out there working to finish off the unloading of the bus and did so until it was done, and that's why you're here today!*

Wow, what a lesson in there for us all. I would like to tell you that I am something special or did something really special that day, but I am not and I did not. I do believe that leadership is in my DNA somehow, and one thing about leaders, and obviously Young Stan saw this in me, is that leaders don't ask others to do what they are unwilling to do themselves. Leaders lead. They lead the way. They serve others. They set examples and they role model their service.

The leader should be the first off the bus and the last still working until the job is complete. When it comes to something personal like the food line, they should be last one in the food line. You take care of your troops first before you take care of yourself. Same goes for any relationship. A husband takes care of his wife before he takes care of himself and a wife takes care of her husband before herself. Seems pretty simple yet too often goes undone or ignored. Young Stan saw leadership potential in me and maybe a good old-fashioned work ethic. It takes one to know one! It takes one to recognize the traits in others.

Young Stan I suspect saw in me what he thought might be a true leader to take charge of this next enterprise. I suspect he thought he saw a leader in this case who believed it his own destiny; his duty and obligation to lead his old team. He recognized that my motivation came from somewhere deep in my soul, not from a place that was looking to have an ego affirmed or just a paycheck paid.

I didn't yet fully appreciate the opportunity that was right in front of me. This was an opening to be with an organization that identified my values as a match to their own. The more we got to know each other, the more we both knew it was right. Stan, knowing how corporate culture works, had me go and meet several times with John Mayasich. With John Mayasich's blessing, there was no way Stan's father, Mr. Hubbard, would veto the decision.

I by no means was totally prepared for this new job. I was too young to know all I needed to know, but I had been mentored by Doug Woog in Junior Hockey and Herb Brooks my first year at the university. I could not have played for two better coaches. Woog was a wonderful teacher, Brooks a master psychologist and chemist. I was mentored by these two excellent coaches, albeit in different ways, which to this day has been an advantage to me in my coaching career. As young as I was when I played for these two great coaches, I was often mindful of the way each worked. I paid attention to all that was happening around me. This I have learned is another trait of a leader—mindful attention to detail. Consequently, I understood more about the way a coach operates than many of my contemporaries.

I had some unique preparation and of course one of the great formulas in life has to do with when preparation meets opportunity. My father got me started. Serratore, Woog, Brooks and others put their mark on me as well. This was it. I again was a lucky man. I did create some of this luck by getting off my butt and unloading the bus and I did pay mindful attention to my coaches those past numbers of years. But it was my formation helped along by other leaders that likely caught the attention of Young Stan. A new opportunity was now right in front of me and for a young guy, I was more prepared than many. And now I had the good fortune of joining a group of world-class leaders and pioneers.

So I got hired. Mr. Hubbard called me into his office shortly thereafter. I knew throughout the process I was not his first choice but he still supported this first decision of Young Stan's. I believe Mr. Hubbard thought I was a bit young and that because the franchise had hit such a low, that maybe an ex-NHL'er with a bigger name might help get the franchise some new traction. I respected that thought.

Never-the-less, here I was—the new coach of the St. Paul Vulcans. So I walked into Mr. Hubbard's office. I was now face to face with a real leader and pioneer and I think I was a little intimidated. Here is what he said to me…leader to leader: *I am going to ask two things of you. I am asking you to never sacrifice your integrity as a coach and never sacrifice the discipline of the team to win a game. If you do these two things, we will never have a problem.* I was expecting to be intimidated by his words, but I was like wow, absolutely, I can do that.

It was inspiring to have this leader and pioneer say simply to me that values mattered. What mattered to him and his organizations was honesty and integrity. He set the bar as far as the value equation goes. This all leaders must do. When values matter, the course is set for good things to happen.

I made mistakes. We will all make mistakes and mistakes are part of any human endeavor. Mistakes need to however be honest mistakes, mistakes that do not sacrifice the values of the team or organization. Mr. Hubbard gave me what was obviously great advice but more importantly, leaders set the bar for what is important. There always needs to be a moral value, a moral compass, or we cannot possibly know what is expected of us or how to behave when something chaotic arises if we do not have that compass to rely on.

Mr. Hubbard went on to ask my opinion about how we might structure some new ideas into the organization, but he was amazingly positive and supportive. He was there to support me! It was another WOW moment in my life and a life lesson from a business pioneer. Values: the why and how we do what we do matters greatly!

That first Vulcan team of my coaching career was successful and went from the previous team being a last place team, to the USHL championship in a single season. Stillwater's Jay Cates and Eric Dornfeld, a goalie tandem in Brad Ryan and Craig Shermoen were on that team...oh I could on and on. Some of the best players I have ever coached played for me that year.

We beat the Sioux City Musketeers in the USHL finals four games to three. The Musketeers were led by one of my favorite coaches of all time, Bob Ferguson. He didn't need this championship; he had the most championships in the history of the league with four. I loved my competition with Fergy. His teams were always a great challenge. Four championships in this highly competitive league is an impressive accomplishment. Fergy set the standard. I was lucky to get one in a head to head with him.

One might think I should be pretty satisfied with a championship in my first year. Mr. Hubbard saw it a little different. I was about to get a very short introduction to staying on top from a very wise leader and pioneer. I don't really think I knew what positive dissent was back then but when I look back, the Hubbard culture loved dissent. If you were in a meeting with them and had an alternative idea, they listened better than any group of people I have ever met. They often asked intelligent and probing questions of your idea or thought.

Now if you were going to offer an alternative idea, you just better know they were going to probe your *why*. You would want to have your idea well thought out, or at least have a good rationale for why you were suggesting such an idea or possible change of course. They were all ears, but they were going to probe.

Anyway, the season was over and we had a dinner celebrating the great season. Mr. Hubbard looked across to his son, Young Stan, and said: *Stanley, great decision on hiring Kevin here.* He looked at me and said: *You know I wasn't sure you were the right guy for us to hire.* Then he looked back at young Stan and continued: *But you did your homework and made a great decision. Congratulations.* Sounded like Young Stan might have had an alternative viewpoint than his dad when this whole thing started! Then he looked back at me, congratulated me as well, and asked if he could share a piece of advice. I of course welcomed it. Mr. Hubbard said, and this one I think I can quote near exactly...he said: *The world's constantly changing and evolving. If you don't change and evolve with it, you'll be left behind.* This again was amazing advice and mentorship from a leader.

Here I sat as a USHL championship coach at the age of 26, younger than any coach in that league. I was being given a nudge to consider all I did that worked in this particular year, but also to understand what leaders know, that some or all of what worked this particular year might not work next year or beyond. We all need to embrace change, positive dissent and innovation, as they are all going to be keys to future successes. I was so lucky to be a part of this family, under their great tutelage and mentorship.

CHAPTER 6:
COURSE CORRECTIONS AND INNOVATION

Have you ever had what you've believed is a good idea, but others seem less than enthused to join in and support it or at least explore it? It can be frustrating for sure. The problem is that for others your good idea is a threat to their way of thinking. It might be a threat to their very way of being. Your idea for a new direction can be taken by some as dismissive of their own ideas or systems they have personally developed. Instead of acknowledging the new idea as a possible positive course correction, a building upon all that was put in place previously, some see it as a threat. These are the types of folks that made famous the saying: *You have got to make them believe it was their idea in the first place*!

The Hubbards, being the great leaders and innovators they were, understood more than most, and certainly more than I did at the time. As you build any industry, you often become a threat to the status quo. You and your new ideas become a threat to those that hold positions in the status quo. In the Minnesota scene, the emergence of Junior Hockey was a threat to the status quo with the status quo being the traditional high school hockey community.

Ron Woodey's idea of Junior Hockey in Minnesota was never intended to replace high school hockey. His vision was to provide another valuable link in the development chain for hockey players in the region. What the Hubbards wanted to do when they bought the Vulcans was to build on Ron's idea to work hand in hand with the current hockey development system. The idea was to first identify the best players graduating from high school not already recruited by the colleges and then give them a legitimate opportunity for continued development through their 20th birthday.

The Hubbards' experience in leadership likely prepared them for potential conflict. I didn't share that experience. I just knew that together we were trying to build a better version of Junior Hockey. Of course building an attractive Junior Hockey option might conflict with the high school model. Some players might opt for the Junior Hockey model over the high school hockey model.

I didn't understand yet how others could look at our good intentions and feel threatened. I was thinking only about how much we were going to help many young men, just as Junior Hockey had helped me. But, as happens with innovation, something new at times replaces something else and there will be conflict. I was about to learn this lesson first hand as such a situation was already on the horizon.

My enlightenment to the conflict innovation can create came immediately in our first year of the new Hubbard ownership. It came in the form of a young player by the name of Shaun Sabol. Shaun was a junior in high school at Minneapolis-South, an inner-city Minneapolis school. South was a very weak school as far as hockey goes. They were non-competitive against the stronger teams. They had one elite player, Shaun, and he had virtually no one else to play with of his caliber. Unknowingly, Shaun was about to take on a leadership and pioneering role of his own, blazing a new trail for others just like him.

It was the first summer of Hubbard Broadcasting ownership with me as the new coach. Many of the returning Vulcan players were playing on the same summer team at Augsburg College's college development league. My plan was to actually coach this summer team and get to know the players who planned to return to the squad. By chance, the late JC Carey who ran Augsburg Ice Arena recommended Shaun to fill out this team's roster. JC, like many others, felt a great desire to help Shaun, as everyone knew what a great and dedicated kid he was. JC thought it would be a good experience for Shaun to be around dedicated players. JC was right.

Shaun played well for our summer team. More importantly, he fell in love with playing with dedicated players. Shaun told me later that summer that he would do anything to play for the Vulcans. His desire was to play with and against good players, not only in games, but in practices as well.

I brought the issue of Shaun wanting to play with us up to the attention of Young Stan and his dad. I knew this would bring into focus a conflict the status quo likely already anticipated—an elite high school player wanting to forego his high school playing days and opting to play juniors instead. This brewing conflict between Junior Hockey and that of the established high school community was going to teach me a lot about how even good ideas and good intentions can pose a threat to some.

Young Stan and his father were in agreement. They instructed me to immediately contact the coaching staff at Minneapolis-South and inform them of Shaun's advances. I did so. After a few meetings with the coaches at the high school and Shaun, it was determined by all, including his high school coaches, that the best place for Shaun was with the Vulcans. His coaches understood this meant a weaker team for them, but out of true concern for Shaun. They knew he needed a stronger challenge.

The South coaches gave Shaun and the Vulcans their blessings to develop together. We worked together to make sure Shaun would get his classes scheduled in the best way possible for him so he could leave school each day in the early afternoon for Vulcan practices. While this development with his high school coaches was a nice surprise, I wasn't wise enough to anticipate the *push back* we would receive from those higher up in the high school hockey establishment.

As we prepared for year one of this new venture together, the Hubbards hosted a group of leaders from the Minnesota hockey community on the Hubbard Broadcasting 132-foot yacht on the St. Croix River. The St. Croix River is a scenic waterway that separates us Viking fans from our archrivals—the Cheese-Heads of Packer Land (the Minnesota/Wisconsin border)! I remember it as a beautiful summer night for a cruise on this pristine waterway. Leaders of our hockey community were well represented. We had a couple of college coaches in attendance. John Mariucci, the god father of U of Minnesota hockey, was there. Seven of the most visible and influential high school coaches attended. Young Stan and his dad were there. John Mayasich was there to represent us too. With Mariucci and Mayasich both on the boat, all we were missing Minnesota legends-wise was Herb Brooks!

Our goal for the evening was to share with these various hockey leaders from around the state of Minnesota the new vision for the franchise as well as for the league and Junior Hockey in general. For example, we explained to the group that there would be academic tutors to help kids with college entrance exams and other resources not before part of the equation. The goal of the Hubbard ownership group was to make a course correction with a serious upgrade in the Vulcan program and in doing so pull the rest of the league upward as well.

As we prepared to share a meal that evening on the boat, the Hubbards gathered all of us in a casual seating area behind the boat's kitchen. The Hubbards gave a summary of what they wanted to improve upon. They articulated their desire to work with everyone to be sure that quality kids were identified and that a quality program was in place to help them achieve their collegiate goals. We wanted all these hockey leaders to leave the boat that night understanding this new and better direction we were committed to providing. The night went mostly well. However I had one sticky issue yet to address.

Before the meeting was over, I brought up the Shaun Sabol situation. I emphasized that our program was not out to recruit high school players away from their high school programs, but in his case, he had legitimate reasons for wanting to play with us. I explained the process we went through with Shaun, even receiving the blessings of his high school coaches. End of story, I thought. Wrong! This was a challenge to the status quo.

Before the night was over, every high school coach on that boat, all seven of them, privately found time to chat with me and asked me to reconsider allowing Shaun to play with us. *Bad precedent* was their message. *This could be detrimental to the high school game* I was told.

I was surprised. I was even maddened to think that these folks were more concerned with a system than this young man. I did not understand how they could not see what I knew to be a purity of intention and motivation to help this young man. We were doing the best we could for Shaun Sabol. How could anyone be against that? I went home befuddled by these leaders of the high school hockey community. It was all so disappointing to me. These were people I looked up to. I didn't know what to think about this. Well, not yet.

It was a great lesson for me in leadership and innovation. It was a clear illustration of the fact that as much as one might think their new path is good, that their motives and goals are honorable, new paths of innovation quite often come as a threat to the status quo. The status quo is often tied to money and even folks' livelihoods. It is tied to ideas nurtured and systems developed. Theirs! I learned that night that no matter one's good intentions and positive innovations, there is going to be resistance by some. And you shouldn't take it personally or even with contempt. It is just a natural part of the process of evolution.

Not everyone is going to welcome your new thought just because you think you are on the side of *right*. The key is to remain focused on your objective, teach, learn, share and evolve. And put all this into action as a service to others. I cannot say that enough. Have a well thought out plan and have it be a service to others. In the end, real leaders also trying to serve others will see what you intend to do and they will either follow in their own way or they will innovate and try an alternative or parallel path.

As it turned out, Shaun was a leader in his own right. He didn't follow the path of the status quo. He sought a new way. He sought a path not travelled by many Minnesotans back then. In his mind, his was a new and better path. Shaun, by the way, played three years for our St. Paul Vulcans, eventually receiving a scholarship to the University of Wisconsin. He became a draft pick of the Philadelphia Flyers. At Madison, Shaun met his wife to be Mindy McClain. I suspect that if you ask Mindy (the daughter of the late Wisconsin football coach Dave McClain), she will confirm that he is dedicated in all he does. I am told that in his real-estate business he was known to sneak BACK to work to get things done, not sneak out of work. Consequently, he built a crazy good real-estate business. Before his Madison based real estate business, Shaun played a number of years of pro-hockey including a brief stint in the NHL with the Flyers. Not bad for a kid from the inner-city with the odds stacked against him.

I was fortunate to be surrounded by great mentors in the world of leadership and not just the Hubbards and John Mayasich. I have mentioned Ron Woodey numerous times. Ron remained with the team as our General Manager during the Hubbard ownership years. Ron was not shy about expressing his views, be they different from yours. He saw his positive dissent as a way to challenge the way of things and helping all around him to become a better version of themselves. He was constantly leading.

I got to know him much better in our coach-General Manager relationship. Ron was tough. He was not shy about telling me that I had issues to correct when he so thought. I recall on several occasions where he told me that I had lost the game with some not so smart personnel moves or how structurally things needed to be changed. I remember one game in particular he was upset and just kind of barged in and told me flat out, *Hartz, you lost the game for us tonight.* He proceeded to tell me why. I always listened to what he had to say and then took what he said and analyzed it. I didn't always agree with him but his critical feedback only served to make me better.

ONE OF THE WORLD'S ALL-TIME GREAT SEVEN-WORD SPEECHES

Ron was never long for words. I still recall maybe the best seven-word speech in the history of the world and it was a speech rooted in leadership to young men. His seven-word speech was a no-nonsense life lesson for all who heard it that day. The story is well worth repeating. He took a slightly different view than most would have ever thought and with it delivered a valuable lesson to all of us in attendance.

As I said earlier, Ron was also a scout for the Philadelphia Flyers, a fact reinforced to all as he often wore a black team leather jacket with a big orange Flyers logo on it. On occasion, Ron would bring Bobby Clarke, Flyers' legend and then General Manager of the Flyers, into our locker-room. They would maybe hang out for a practice and so on. Having Bobby Clarke visit our locker room was always a treat for our boys. Everyone knew of Ron's love and loyalty to the Flyers. We all felt a little kinship or at least a little extra interest in the Flyer organization. Our most famous alumni, Paul Holmgren, was a player with the Flyers back then and today is their team President.

One year, a tragic event occurred within the Flyers organization. Their young goaltender, Pelle Lindbergh, a native of Stockholm, Sweden, and a Vezina Trophy winner, the trophy awarded to the NHL's best goaltender, died late one night after crashing his car. He was said to have had an affinity for fast cars and also for driving them fast. My recollection of the Pelle Lindbergh story that night is that it was a late-night thing and in some manner with both alcohol and high speed involved, Pelle had gotten reckless and basically killed himself because of his reckless driving. He crashed into a barrier of some kind. The news became very public very quickly and there was no shortage of media inferring that Pelle killed himself being reckless.

Of course our team knew how much Ron loved the Flyers and Pelle was their young Vezina Trophy-winning star of the team. Our boys and staff were concerned with how Ron was taking the news. Some of our players asked me before practice that next day how Mr. Woodey was doing, but I hadn't seen him yet. He showed up near the end of practice and I approached him and gave him my condolences and asked if he would address the team as they were concerned with how he was doing. He said he would.

At the end of practice, I gathered the team and shared with them that Mr. Woodey would address them regarding Pelle.

The boys, in a more hurried manner than usual, got everything and everybody off the ice and to the locker room to hear what Mr. Woodey had to say.

I recall grabbing an open stall in the locker room as Ron walked in. I recall how respectfully quiet the boys were. I recall that Ron had on his famous Flyers black leather jacket. He walked slowly from one end of the room to the other, and back again and then back again not uttering a word. For what seemed minutes, he paced and all the time with his hands tucked in his jacket pockets in deep thought. It remained dead quiet in the room as Ron seemed to struggle with what to say. Then he gave the great seven-word speech. Ron finally, slowly and deliberately uttered somewhat softly for him: *One man's misfortune… is another man's fortune.* His speech was over and he left the room. WOW, I thought to myself!

So typical this was of Ron. He thought about his audience; these young aspiring hockey players. He thought about what mattered to them. He thought about how to best serve them. He then cut right to the heart of the issue as far as the message he wanted to deliver to these young men. He couldn't make excuses for a young and popular NHL star as by all accounts it was his own recklessness that killed him. He shared with them the way things were, at least from his perspective.

Ron had a knack for being brief and to the point, no gray areas and little room for concern over someone's feelings. That was his leadership style. Honest even if it meant with sharp edges. One always knew what Ron thought and he never pulled his punches. He is one of the reasons I have been lucky to be involved in hockey as long as I have been. When Ron passed away I felt extremely honored that his wife Eleanor asked me to speak at his funeral. He was a hockey pioneer and leader.

HORSE SENSE

Leaders surrounded me. Jerry Griffith, a volunteer assistant coach with me during my Vulcan years, was another. Jerry owned a glass shop in White Bear Lake. I played Gopher hockey with his son Steve who was also a 1984 Olympian. Jerry is one of those guys who coached his kids and many others as they grew through the youth hockey ranks. Getting to know Jerry is getting to see and hear common old "horse sense" at its finest. I knew he was loaded with horse sense and I wanted him around to teach me. Jerry was a mentor I sought out. Being he had his own business, I didn't have to pay him much, which was good because I didn't have anything to pay him. Still, he took the challenge on and mentored our team and me as often as his time would allow.

Jerry was an incredible mentor and leader. He spent many years of volunteer coaching in the Roseville youth hockey association. He saw firsthand how often the problems of a child were developed in the home and from the adults in his life. In our first year with our new Vulcan team I recall Jerry telling me during a team dinner, *I'll tell you all you need to know about a kid by the way he eats at the dinner table. Really*, I said. *Yes, really,* he said. *It's a matter of parenting and what kind of parenting is taking place at the dinner table.* Jer continued, *What kind of leadership does the parent show the child and in the end, does the child learn to show respect, do they say 'please pass the potatoes', or are they unconcerned for others at the table?*

That was the gist of it and as he was telling me this. Darned if one of our young players from another table interrupts us. I think this young lad shouted over a question about when the bus was leaving from lunch. I remember Jerry immediately recognizing the very offense he was talking about as he turned to me and said, *There you go...THAT kid's going to be a problem. See how he didn't know how to show respect?*

This young man interrupted us without concern for us and our conversation at the dinner table. Jerry pointed it out and he stated immediately that this was the very illustration of what he was mentoring me on. I recall thinking...o*k, Mr. Fortune Teller, we'll see*! Long story short, Jerry was 100% right. This young man was a problem child with problem parents who did not make it through the season with us.

One future day not that long after this young man quit and left our team, I witnessed this boy's parents putting on a display of irrational behavior at a hockey event unlike anything I have ever seen out of a set of parents. Jer recognized this family dynamic right at the lunch table that day.

Jerry mingled throughout the locker room with sayings like *the problem is not that you have to get out of bed so early in the morning, it's that you stay up too late at night. Got to be willing to change as what you are today is not what your potential is. Welcome these difficult challenges and know this game and this life are only going to get harder...but the more difficult the challenge the sweeter the rewards.* That is one thing we don't seem to want to tell our youth but it is true; life only gets more challenging. It doesn't get easier; it gets harder. Of course the rewards can be pretty incredible too. But there is a price to paid, a saying that Jerry said more often than any other, *"You've got to be willing to pay the price!"* We all know anything worth having has a price attached to it.

Jerry would often play *good cop* with our young players after I had been hard on them telling them, *"When someone who cares about you tells you about your faults, when you receive personal criticism you should thank them, not run away from them...they simply care and want to make you better."* We all know that learning to accept criticism is part of any process of improvement. This concept is not always easy for young people and especially young gifted athletes who have had much given to them in the way of God-given talents. They are often spoiled by the very nature of their natural gifts. The key of course is to recognize our gifts and give them the mindful attention they need to be developed to their potential. Jerry was often simply reinforcing what many young people had heard from their parents. Our team members and I were lucky to have Jerry in our lives.

Bottom line is leadership starts at home with parents and community leaders. Leadership needs to be role-modeled every day by the adults in the community. We are too often lacking in this area, but again, it is our own fault as a society. We need to regain a focus on the nurturing of leadership so its values have a better chance to be handed down from generation to generation.

CHAPTER 7:
VALUES MATTER

All great leadership begins with a set of values that are then put into the service of others. Leaders and followers have to first know *why* we all want to act in the first place. And when we look at great leaders we usually know exactly *what* they stood for. For example, we all know what Martin Luther King stood for. That is what we know most about him! We don't necessarily know which church Dr. King attended weekly or a host of other facts. However, we do know the values for which he stood. Those who shared in Dr. King's vision and values followed him or led in other ways, but with the same values as their driving force.

If you want to be happy in your work life, find organizations in which you share their values. I was lucky...I was involved in such an organization when I joined Hubbard Broadcasting. I loved their values and understood this was an organization I could thrive in. After six great years of coaching the Vulcan hockey team, the Hubbard family offered me a higher level of opportunity within their great organization. As a husband and a father to a very young and growing family, I had to take advantage of the opportunity. The financial opportunities were substantially better than what I could find in the hockey industry. Many people pay colleges thousands of dollars for educations in business, ethics, leadership and overall professional knowledge. In working at Hubbard Broadcasting, I was getting paid a salary and getting a great education at the same time.

The Hubbards were not only running great media companies but were embarking on a pioneering project that would come to be known as Direct-TV. They did all they did under an umbrella of values. They exposed values of honesty, integrity, service to others and hard work. How could I lose by saying yes to the higher-level opportunity?

My experiences at Hubbard Broadcasting will go down as my best professional years. To be involved with so many great leaders and innovators and eventually to be part of a high-end, extremely professional sales team was a tremendous experience. For ten years I was part of a smart, super professional and hard working sales team. The KSTP-TV sales team I was a part of was as professional as they come, and the fundamentals of running great teams don't change from one organization or one sport to another. Like a hockey team, we had our high-priced, high-end talent on our sales team. The top successful and compensated executives expected better and more than most. Like a highly compensated goal-scorer, they could be fickle, but it was most often in the name of the pursuit of excellence. Top professionals understand that excellence is a value, and a value that brings with it financial rewards.

High-end talent is often high-end because it doesn't think like average talent. Whether it be hockey or industry, the talented leaders are constantly looking at new ideas, formulating new strategies and taking paths that others won't. Hockey coaches know this too—their best players don't often fit into the team as uniformly as other *everyday* players. The best players often see the game differently. Can you imagine a coach telling a young Wayne Gretzky that he is to do everything just like all his other teammates? That might include being instructed not to hang around behind the opponent's net because no one else hangs around the back of the opponent's net. Gretzky saw it differently and became of one the first players to make his home office in the space behind the opponent's net. Sales talent is no different.

Gerry Brouwer was an ex-track star at the University of Minnesota and probably the most highly compensated sales executive on our team. He was one of our star players. I was instructed to shadow him in my first weeks on my new sales team. To shadow means I simply followed him wherever he went to observe and learn. I watched, listened and learned.

The story I most remember is of a morning when Gerry and I walked into our boss's office (with me trailing, of course) and I basically watched as Gerry gave more than a little constructive criticism to our boss, local sales manager Mike Wagonner. At first it seemed to me to be an unusual occurrence—the star player on the sales team in effect giving the coach some edgy and critical feedback. But I needed to see this. In the world of sports from where I grew up, the coach and leader talked *at* the players.

I needed to see a great organization in action from this new perspective. In a great organization with great leadership, the leaders are listeners and gatherers of information from their troops. I learned that day about what valuable sources of information to managers and leaders are those who work for them and for the organization.

That day Gerry was basically telling our boss that he had not been provided the tools and information he needed to effectively get the job done. There were missing parts to the plan...in his estimation. Gerry was prepared with his rationale, and he gave our sales manager (our boss) various reasons for his point of view. More importantly, our boss Mike Wagonner listened intently to Gerry. Mike's job of course was to use Gerry's feedback to make a better and more comprehensive plan in order to better arm his sales team with the tools they needed to more effectively perform their jobs.

For me in the coaching world, I hadn't yet been exposed to such strong feedback from the team or a team member. I had certainly gotten feedback from time to time, but not like this. My younger men back with the Vulcans either didn't know or were too intimidated to bring unsolicited feedback to their boss. Maybe I wasn't smart enough or experienced enough to ask for their feedback in the right ways. I would be sure to change that in my future managing duties which were going to include a return to coaching hockey. But on this day, I was surprised to see a team member share such hard criticism with his superior. It was a lesson on how leaders listen to their troops and seek to gain from their feedback and knowledge in an effort to improve the overall organization.

The individuals on this great sales team brought great feedback to our bosses every week in our sales meetings. It was the job of the coach and manager to put all our feedback together and bring the team better tools and strategies for getting the job done. I am pretty sure that elite quarterbacks like Peyton Manning and Tom Brady bring their coaching staffs feedback on what they see, what they expect out of certain situations. The coaches then have to create a plan to take advantage of the talents and vision of their quarterbacks and other players on the team. The coach's or manager's job is simply to put each player on the team in the best possible position for individual and team success.

Leaders bring valuable ideas and direction to their team. Leaders also listen in an effort to improve process and serve others.

Examples of great teamwork and leadership abounded daily at Hubbard Broadcasting. A few years later when I had become more established in the KSTP-TV Sales Department, the new Mariucci Arena was being built to be the new home of Gopher Hockey. As a Gopher Hockey alumni, I volunteered to be part of a small committee that was charged with opening the new arena with a bang. I was fortunate to work with this small group of great people, including then current head hockey coach Doug Woog, along with Jan Unstad and Nancy Hankinson from the Gopher Athletic Department.

Our task was to put together a Golden Gopher Alumni game(s) to open the new arena in style! Plans were formulated to have an old-timers game which was to be followed by a newer-timers game. Players past and present were to be the first to skate on the ice. The history of Gopher Hockey was to be on display on one evening for all to see. It was a pretty easy concept to sell.

To make a long story short, I offered to the committee use of my position at Hubbard Broadcasting to access the media portals within the Minnesota media community to get the word out and get the arena full of Gopher supporters. Many of the resources we needed were right there in-house at Hubbard Broadcasting. And if you knew the Hubbard family, you knew they were great supporters of the University of Minnesota.

I went to Young Stan Hubbard with the *what's* and *why's* of my task and our committee's ideas. I remember vividly Young Stan saying to me, *just tell us how we can help you.* I remember thinking he trusted me to get it done and he was now at my service to help me. He and the resources of the Hubbard organization would be at my disposal. Leaders lead, and leaders know when to follow and support or even when to get out of the way. Young Stan empowered me to get the job done.

I went to the head of the Hubbard Broadcasting Art Department, as I had some artist's renditions of what the finished Mariucci Arena was going to look like. When I asked the department head for her help, she said, "Oh, this is the Gold Star project I heard about." A Gold Star project I was about to find out meant that the leadership within the company had informed all the department heads within Hubbard Broadcasting of my task and that they should find every means possible to help me complete the task. They were all at *my* service.

We proceeded to make some print boards for print advertising and also for use in radio and TV spots. We shared these with other media outlets in the market. We constructed radio and television promotional spots in a way that each local media outlet if they so desired, could put their own voice and face to it to make it seem their own. We made it easy for them to personalize it and promote the great event. Our fellow media throughout the Twin Cities totally supported the effort as everyone shared in the goal of promoting our hometown college and the opening of the new arena. Gopher Sports and Gopher Hockey are a staple of our community, and the opening of the new arena was a big event for everyone. The opening of the arena and the two alumni games were a huge success. The leadership expertise I was exposed to, again with the Hubbard family, was second to none.

LEADERS SERVE THEIR TEAMS, THEIR TEAM MEMBERS, THEIR COMMUNITIES, AND OTHERS

As a side note to my fellow hockey fans, I had a couple of personal highlights from those alumni games. One was seeing John Mayasich on the ice. Many had never seen him play (his career was before TV and videotape). When I first let John know we expected him to play, he said that he was just too old... I explained that the old-timers game was where he would play and Gopher Hockey had to have John Mayasich on the ice. John obliged. The second highlight was a scoring play in the newer-timers game. It was announced on the new PA system that scoring for team Gold is Broten, from Broten and Broten. Three brothers together on one scoring play; that was pretty cool! And the arena was full. Full. It was a great showcase for the tradition of Gopher Hockey and the beginning of a new history in the new Mariucci Arena. The Hubbard family and their team members had quietly done their part.

I've learned a lot from the Hubbards and others, and one thing I am convinced of is that success starts at the top. You or I can bring all the right values to a job or mission, but if the leaders we report to don't share the same values in leadership or honesty or whatever the values are that we find important, they cannot possibly appreciate those values in our work.

If top management's values don't match yours, you'll too often go home frustrated and wondering what is wrong with them when it is simply a *disconnect* in how you each view the world. My advice to young job-seekers: When you go to an interview, never forget you are interviewing them as well. Why are they in this business or endeavor? Not just *what* do they expect from you, but find out *why* they expect the things of you that they do. Additionally, find out what their values are in achieving the tasks they will charge you with.

If you are in the position of manager hiring team members, do the same and find those future employees who believe in what your organization is doing and how they do it. If in the end you want motivated employees and team members, find those that believe in your mission and values; you'll never have to worry about motivating them.

The Hubbards wanted all their teams to win of course. They wanted their news teams to win ratings battles, sales teams to maximize revenue, and their hockey team to win as many games as possible, but only with honor and only with integrity. Winning any other way was against their core values. They understood better than most that winning over the long haul is a by-product of doing many things right and values are a big part of that winning formula. There can be no shortcuts for success. I could never be happy working for someone who didn't want it that way. With the Hubbard family, I could be successful and have my efforts recognized. That is why it has been said over and again by many that for successful teams and organizations: *Success starts at the top by establishing values and expectations for all team members.*

I have heard one too many times someone say, "They pay my salary, I've got to be loyal to them." That, my friends, is a bunch of B.S. If you allow your loyalty to be defined by money and/or a paycheck, you will be too easily manipulated to do something maybe totally against your value system. First and foremost you owe your loyalty to a set of values that really matter!

I suspect many individuals could have fixed many of the scandals we read about in the news media. Maybe they were afraid of dissent and conflict or they just didn't know what value sets were important. This is poor leadership within that organization or group. Workers within the system should be empowered to speak up based upon knowledge and values. Ask the questions that matter before we hire or before we get hired. Like Mr. Hubbard did with me, he set the platform and expectations for core values like honesty and positive dissent. Our teams and individuals will still make mistakes but they will be honest mistakes, the kind we can all live with.

FIGHT FOR VALUES

Some people talk about *having your back*. That means that when the going gets tough and in the face of conflict, teammates and communities will support you, and you them. Folks won't think twice about this when they share values. Societies will go to war and die for one another when they share the same values and find those values important. At Hubbard Broadcasting, where most shared the same value sets, we could often stand together to face a problem. Here is another real-life example of what you can expect when you join forces with folks who share your values.

Eventually I became the National Sales Manager for KSTP-TV. It was an awesome responsibility. I managed a network of professionals responsible for tens of millions of dollars in sales revenues. Those revenues sustained jobs and the families dependent on those jobs. It was a responsibility I took seriously.

My direct boss was a wonderful man by the name of Karl Gensheimer. Karl was a German immigrant who as a young boy was sent by his family to America to avoid the many dangers of Germany during World War II. He was a tough-minded German man, who many years later is still sporting a mid to heavy German accent. I continue to love this man today. He knew our industry well and expected a high level of professionalism from our team.

As National Sales Manager, like everyone in sales, I had that one tough client who at times would drive one to wonder why they even attempt to get out of bed in the morning. This particular buyer controlled a lot of money, more money than any other client we worked with at the TV station. It was Christmastime, and she wanted our station to attempt something new, a new format for a commercial for one of her strong Christmastime clients. I said I would look into it.

TV and its commercial breaks have a lot of structure. The local commercial breaks have to line up with national commercial breaks and so on. It is not so easy to manipulate commercial breaks, and our folks who control that kind of thing told me that in the short time before Christmas would arrive, I had no chance to make it happen. They also told me that it likely never would happen.

I shared this with my tough at times to work with buyer and she put up a heck of a storm. She told me how other TV stations and many in other markets (other cities) were making it happen. So in the name of due diligence and service to my client, I continued to *dig* and see if I could get this done for her. I thought I might learn from others how they were getting it done, so I called a couple National Sales Managers in other markets that I knew also worked with this buyer to try and learn about how they were making this happen. Two fellow NSM's from other markets basically told me that to get this tough old buyer off their back, they just lied to her. They told her they would get it done, but we all knew that with the structure of TV breaks that it wasn't going to happen. They told me to just tell her you'll do it, she'll forget about it and it will all go away. I couldn't do that.

I couldn't share with my buyer that her other NSM's in the other markets were lying to her. I shared with this tough buyer that after further due diligence and research that we just could not accommodate her and her client. She became threatening. She controlled not only this money, but a lot of money for other clients as well. She let me know I was jeopardizing that other money as well. This was not a professional thing to do on her part—to use other client's budgets as a weapon in this negotiation. She literally told me I was stupid and thought there was something wrong with me as the other markets were getting it done. She continued to insinuate that this would *cost us*.

I had to share this issue with my boss Karl. I could not at some point have one of our most influential buyers and customers mad at me and have Karl blindsided not knowing about it. I gave Karl a full report. After Karl got the report from me, he immediately got on the phone with this buyer (with me sitting in front of him) and told her in no uncertain terms that she ought to appreciate her hard-working NSM (which was me). He went on to tell her that I went to bat for her within our TV station and did the extra homework in other markets. Bottom line, he told her that sometimes the answer is no, it cannot be done, and that he suspected that no one in any other market could get it done either. He also went on to give her a little extra, telling her how our commitment to honest work and integrity should not be threatened but should be valued and appreciated. Karl had my back. He would not allow her to treat me with anything but respect, as that is how we treated her. I couldn't believe how forceful he was...well, knowing Karl, maybe I can believe it!

He definitely had my back and to my surprise, this buyer totally backed down. I cannot tell you how good it feels to know someone has your back. The lesson here however is that teammates and bosses are only going to have your back if you all share the same values. If money was the only value in this example, this could have played out differently. Leadership and values are intertwined.

Anyone who knew me believed that I would never leave Hubbard Broadcasting. I loved it there. But always looking for a new challenge, I got an offer to help another company. They gave me a modest piece of equity in the company and eventually I became their CEO. It was a small company with just six owners. I learned in a hurry that being a CEO is quite a tough job. Of these six owners, they all had different views of the world, with different value sets on how a company should be run. It might be the only job ever had that I did not enjoy. But it was my own fault. I would explore a group like this better next time and would make better decisions based upon the values that each member held. That said, we sold the company...in part because the ownership group had such different views on how to move the business forward. In the end, it was a good experience for me and I moved on to find the next great challenge.

A short time later, a good friend (and excellent business talent) of mine, Scott Jahnke, and I bought a small hockey company called Proguard Sports. He and I and our families continue to be good partners to this day. Being a partner in this business allowed me to get back to my main passion, and that is coaching. This time, however, I was more equipped than ever before to teach the game, the teamwork that is needed in the game, and leadership. If the right opportunity came, I would jump at it.

Through a series of events, I was put together with the Sioux Falls Stampede. Local owner Gary Weckwerth and majority owner Bill Sexton were great people with great values. When the opportunity came, I was excited to get back after it, though this time I was better equipped on a lot of levels. The opportunity in Sioux Falls fit my *why*...the why I get out of bed every day. In Junior Hockey I could help do for others what Junior Hockey had done for me. I always felt the coach at the junior level could have a great and positive influence on his players. Coaching at this level brings with it an awesome responsibility, one I took very seriously and was eager to get back after. This time I was bringing more knowledge about helping teams develop and helping individuals reach their potential. Values and leadership would be at the forefront of all we were about to do. I had been mentored by some of the best. I was ready...

PART THREE: LEADERSHIP LESSONS

CHAPTER 8:
GREAT TEAMS = LEADERSHIP AND GREAT TEAMMATES

THE 2005-2006 SIOUX FALL STAMPEDE

The Mad-House on Hickman was energized and we were ready to take the ice. I had been part of a National Championship team as college player. I had coached a National Champion in this very league. I had also been a member and eventually a team leader with a great sales team in the television industry, but this team in Sioux Falls was extra special.

With fifteen years of being mentored and mentoring in leadership roles, I was now more equipped than ever before to be a good coach-teacher and leader of these young men. But it wasn't me and my experiences that made this journey to this game so special. The truth is I was again going to be mentored by a special group of coaches and young players. I suspect I played some part in what was an incredible team experience in winning a franchise record of 43 regular season games, but this team wasn't about me. It was about them. This special night, this special year had to do exactly with the team!

There is no question that this team of coaches and players were a special mix; maybe a once-in-a-lifetime mix of talent and humble desire. Nothing replaces a group of teammates who truly want to be collectively great and are willing to sacrifice for one another. That was this team.

This night was a convergence of much of what I hold dear. The game of hockey was one of those things I hold dear. I love hockey because the sport preaches as its most important value the importance of individual character and commitment to

team. It is a brotherhood. It is about service to the person next
to you in the locker room or *the room* as it is called. That said,
a true total commitment by all team members is still hard to
find.

Also on this night, the game about to be played is a showcase
of young but high-end talent. The United States Hockey
League (USHL) is the showcase for this talent. It continues to
be a wonder of a league. Most American-born, college-bound
athletes play their sports in their hometowns for their high
school teams. We see this of course in basketball, football and
baseball as the main feeders of talent to the NCAA universities.
This is not the rule of things in hockey. Hockey in America is
now a nationwide sport, but when it comes to development of
our elite talent, the USHL has no rival. Many of the best
hockey talent in America spends their formative development
time in towns in Iowa, Nebraska, North and South Dakota and
more, to play and develop in the only Tier 1 Junior League in
America, the USHL. It has become bigger than I think even
Ron Woodey could have ever envisioned.

The Des Moines Ice Arena, The Madhouse on Hickman is
rocking with excitement. The franchise itself is a storied one in
Junior Hockey. It has been around a long time and its storied
past had developed a loyal fan base. The arena's old lighting
system is not up to the standards of the new arenas around the
country. The dim aura and wooden bench seats painted in the
home team's colors of blue and red, give the arena an
immediate feel of going back in time to an era when arenas
were dark from the smoke-filled air. An old and broken-down
visitors locker room, that often holds too much humidity even
in the cold months of a northern plains winter, are now in the
spring of the year during play-off time, too warm and humid to
be comfortable. But you make do.

By this time of the season, these young players have already
grown hardened. Hardened to how tough this game of hockey
is. Most don't arrive to the league so. I have always
appreciated the description of the USHL as shared with me by
Kevin Holmstrom, a father of two boys from Colorado Springs,
Ben (one of two captains of this team) and Josh who would

play for us a few years later. Josh would also serve as a captain for us in Sioux Falls. Their father Kevin simply describes the league in one word—unforgiving.

Think of this as a parent. You have a son who is obviously a very fine hockey player. He often already has a Division I scholarship commitment to one of America's finest universities. This boy is living an American dream. He then trots off to the USHL either as a high school student, or an 18/19-year-old high school graduate, to get a lesson in the real world of hockey before going on to the college of his choice. What he and his family find is at times an unkindly and unforgiving test. They find out in a hurry that the real world of hockey is very hard. Each boy's deficiencies will be exposed quickly and for all to see. Each will also be asked to do a man's job for which most are not yet socially or physically equipped. As Kevin Holmstrom describes it, an *unforgiving* experience!

It is an especially great challenge for outstanding athletes who have been told in their respective hometowns how special they and how special their talents are. When they get to the USHL their talents usually are not more special than anyone else's. Their talents are closer to the normal. Whatever talents they do have had better be accompanied by a strong will and work ethic, because they will be tested on many levels by competition not only from their opposition, but from the internal competition within their team. I have often compared this test of Junior Hockey to a trade school that crosses the boundaries of both a military boot camp and a sports academy. Players will leave this experience with a different worldview.

As a parent, if you had Kevin Holmstrom's perspective, his understanding of the unforgiving nature of this military-like trade school experience awaiting your son, you and your son(s) had a better chance to succeed. What was at first a new and exciting experience was going to turn to unforgiving. When the going got tough, those families who understood going in how hard this experience was going to be, had a better chance of helping their son to navigate the struggle. It helps to have a family to understand this going in so they can provide the right kind of emotional support and leadership to their young son living away from home. No matter how often we told families in the initiation process how hard the experience was going to be, most families did not appreciate this reality.

We all know the saying *when the going gets tough, the tough get going*. That is the USHL. That is why college coaches often want their players to play in this league before heading off to their college. The lessons the players acquire in this unforgiving league will in most cases allow these young men to develop the necessary tools needed to be ready to contribute as freshmen at their universities. The experience will toughen them; it will harden them...if they are able to embrace the challenge.

The strong survive to be very good college players and even professionals. The strong also populate very good college hockey teams. In 2011-12, over one third of all NCAA Division I hockey programs were made up of USHL alums. When the NCAA conducted their national tournament, the NCAA final 16, USHL alums accounted for 51 percent of all participants. That is a statistically significant increase from the 33% or so that make up all D-1 teams. When it came to the quality teams, the percentage of USHL alums populating those teams increased substantially. They did so because these are boys who had met the challenge of the unforgiving USHL. They were *battle-tested-tough*!

NO ENTITLEMENTS

When your stars and leaders are humble and committed to the team, you have a great chance to succeed. Likewise, you show me a humble and great leader of a business team and I'll show you a great team.

The special nature of this night had to do with many factors but none more so than the people themselves. This collective group of people was all I envisioned a great team to be. They were humble; they each wanted to do their part to win. They shared team and individual values. And if I remember correctly, we were picked to finish last!

It was the group, the team that made this journey to this night so special. Sharing any experience with strength, conditioning, life-coach Kevin Ziegler is special. I have never, and I mean never, met a coach or manager who works so hard and selflessly for the betterment of the team and each individual on the team. Kevin takes the ideal of coach and servant to a level I have not experienced before of since. Kevin has coached (strength and conditioning) at the NHL level, and he understands more than most not only what it takes to get to that level, but what a great teammate looks like. Not only was he a great resource in the area of strength, conditioning, nutrition and the like, but he *walked our walk and talked our talk*. We shared the values of service to our players.

We talked about this that very first night together when considering working together. I think Kevin at that time had gown weary of the NHL scene, one often dominated by individual wants and desires…and egos! I knew from my time with the Hubbards, that finding those that share your values was a key to success. Kevin and I knew it right away when we met that we shared the same values. We both knew what was important to us and we knew we shared the values of honest service to our players and integrity in all we do. We shared many hockey ideals too and the concept of leadership. We were a great team, he and I. Kevin says to this day, he will work only with those who share his values, which he and I did. Unfortunately, he knows as I do that it can be hard to find.

Love is a concept brought to athletics, to my recollection anyway, first by Vince Lombardi. He spoke of loving your teammates; respecting their growth and ambitions. Kevin Ziegler epitomizes this. His whole world epitomizes love and selflessness. His actions speak every day about how to better those around him. He never rests on yesterday's accomplishments, never allows himself to believe what he did yesterday was good enough for today. He shows his belief in leadership values by role-modeling them every day. As Mr. Hubbard shared with me those early years with the Vulcans: *The world is constantly changing and evolving, you change and evolve with it, or you will be left behind*. In the case of Kevin Ziegler, he lives this value every day. He was constantly searching for the most up to date and innovative knowledge, not for his own ego but because he knew this was the best way to serve the young athletes he was destined to work with. He was always searching for ways to help each athlete become a better version of themselves. There is no finer coach or person that I have ever worked with. To be going through this battle together with Z, on this night, was special.

Coach Doug Schueller is one of the finest people you will ever meet and an outstanding coach. He was a strong-willed player in his day. He was a captain of his Junior team and a captain at Bowling Green University. He exuded leadership from his very being. Not only is Doug an excellent coach (now the head coach at St. Johns University), but again a person who believes in the values we were all preaching together. Like Z, going through the journey with a fellow coach you could absolutely count on, made this evening more special.

This particular group of players that we coaches were able to serve made this journey most special. As a group, they may have been the most unspoiled and hungry group of athletes I have ever been around. All seemed to have had some adversity in their recent careers. All had been humbled. This was a true team of young men who wanted to win and all of whom wanted to play for each other. They simply wanted to help create a great experience for the teammate sitting next to them! Often said, not as often realized!

Their journeys were not of the easy variety and they embraced this challenge like no other team I have ever coached. Please remember this group was picked to finish last! But individually and collectively they embraced hard. There was no jealousy of teammate's success. They were not focused on the rewards for self. Our cast of characters was not a lineup of the chosen or the privileged; these were kids who were more from the school of hard knocks and they displayed a sense of team every day. In that regard, they were a coach's dream and I was so happy to be a part of it.

We had already won the Anderson Cup, the trophy for the best record over the regular season. In Junior Hockey I think winning the regular season championship is more important than it is for other leagues and levels. Since the USHL is a development league for college and professional players, it shows the various professional and university scouts what a player can do over the longer haul. A great regular season brings attention to the individuals on the team and allows for a better recruiting platform for those players not yet committed to the various college levels. So the season had already been a great success. Our pursuit of the play-off championship was just one more challenge for a group of young men who had embraced the challenge together all year long. It is worth repeating: This was a group predicted by most to finish dead last.

In the end, what made this journey special was the special room we had. The *room*, as they call it in hockey, is the chemistry of the players in the locker room. You cannot fake chemistry. Positive chemical reactions come when a team has solid leadership and a group of committed teammates, all committed to the bigger picture of team success.

GRIT

What this team had above all else was grit! I saw a great presentation from a Stanford professor on TED, a website dedicated to the mission of sharing great ideas. The professor's subject matter was that of grit being a predictor of a person's future success. Through her various studies she came to the conclusion that grit is the only real predictor of future success. Grit, not IQ or social economic status or anything else she had studied, is a better predictor of future success. I have no trouble believing that.

I define grit as the ability and desire to overcome adversity. It is the desire to face challenges, to face a difficult challenge and overcome whatever obstacles are in the way of success. I think in the end the development of personal grit comes from adversity in one's life and learning how to cope with it. People with grit usually have had some challenges in their lives and they have simply figured out how to overcome those challenges or at least not give into the adverse situation presented them.

This Sioux Falls Stampede team was loaded with kids with grit. These boys embraced each challenge. At no point did this team feel any sense of entitlement. This group felt they already had overcome much just to get to each incremental success and were willing to take on whatever was needed to get past the next hurdle that was sure to be put in their way. This group of athletes was full of grit and selflessness.

To see what a special group loaded with grit looks like, let's start with our two captains, both of who are playing or have played at times in the National Hockey League. Nate Prosser is from Elk River, MN and currently plays for the Minnesota Wild. He made what in Minnesota is an unpopular choice when he chose to leave his high school for his senior year to seek a harder challenge than the Minnesota High School system had to offer him. He had lofty expectations for himself when he left his high school as a senior. Yet two years later he had played on two pretty poor Junior teams in Sioux Falls and was being scheduled for a third. Two years of losing was not to his liking and having league polls predicting a last-place finish was not what he had envisioned. He was tired of losing.

His captain counterpart Benny Holmstrom might be the ultimate captain. He is from Colorado Springs, CO. He has played some for the Philadelphia Flyers but spends most of his playing days in the AHL. He came to the USHL just before his teammate Prosser, but had injuries off and on in the previous two seasons and without question, wanted to play a full year and desperately wanted to win. For the two seasons he shared with his good friend Nate Prosser, Ben was rarely healthy. Like Nate, he was sick of losing.

The thing about these two young men, both of whom went on to be captains at their respective colleges, Prosser at Colorado College and Holmstrom at the University of Massachusetts Lowell, is you could not ever meet two more dedicated young men. And by dedicated, I mean not only to themselves, but also to their team.

In the case of Benny, he was in his third season in Sioux Falls when I arrived to coach. I saw great value in Benny's game. But the value I saw led to the kind of roles that often do not get your name in the headlines. Benny got all the greasy roles on the team. If we were up a goal late in a game, or killing penalties, or needed a shot blocked, you can be sure Benny was on the ice. When power-play time came, when the guys who score the goals and earn the attention of the newspaper headlines were in the game, Benny was often sitting pretty close to me on the bench. Three hard years in the league and his new coach had him in the *grease-pile*, doing all the dirty work. Benny did much of the work that doesn't get the headlines. But he embraced his role, and he did it with enthusiasm. He did it for the team. He did it for the guy sitting next to him in the locker room whom he truly cared about. And he did it because he believed it would lead to team success.

Ben Holmstrom performed so well in the *grease-pile,* and without complaint, that he gave no one else on the team a platform for complaint. How could a first-year player complain about anything when they watched Benny, our third-year player, leader and captain, take care of the *grease-pile*? Oh, Benny will tell you about the day he and his line did got to go out on the power-play and of course they scored. *One for one on the power-play*, he would remind me! But he reminded me with a smile and he fought hard for his team every day.

I caught up with Benny in August of 2012 as he prepared to start his season in the American Hockey League with the Adirondack Phantoms, the top minor league affiliate of the Philadelphia Flyers. In the past couple of years he has gotten called up to the Philadelphia Flyers from time to time, and when he is sent back to their top farm team in Adirondack, he wears the Captain "C". I am not surprised. He is a special person. I told him this was the one team I wanted to write about in this book and he told me immediately and with enthusiasm: *Coach, it was my favorite year of hockey I have ever had!* I was pleasantly surprised to hear such a positive first response.

Why, I asked him, why was that Stampede team the most enjoyable team he had ever played on? Benny went on to say: *We had the best blend of players you could ever want, everyone bought into the team being successful. We had a common goal*

*and the selfish individual goals did not get in the way. I have
not since come across a team anything like that one.*

Now here is a guy who I believe was the youngest captain in
the American Hockey League in 2011. He was a three-year
captain at the U of Massachusetts Lowell. He may be the most
naturally gifted hockey player I have come across, but a
stronger captain you will never find. When I asked him where
this leadership gift came from, he really didn't know. I know
he admires his parents (and I do as well), but I think he felt like
it was a natural thing for him. He said he played for his coach-
dad up until his high school-midget hockey years and there was
always a lot expected of him. That said, he loved to work hard
and that made him a role model for others.

Hard work is attractive in any field and it is especially
attractive in the game of ice hockey, a game where luck at
times plays a little bigger role in the outcome of a game night
after night than most other sports. Great plays happen, but luck
in hockey happens too. Therefore, it is incumbent on a player
to go out and work as hard as possible to create as much good
luck as possible. A hockey player cannot get lucky if not in the
right place at the right time. Benny is all about that. He is a
hard worker and fierce competitor for sure.

Make no mistake; there is something different about this young
man. He has physical talent, but not the physical talent of some
of his upper-tier peers. Benny is what we call, in hockey, a
grinder. He plays with grit and determination, and in the
hockey world, there is a place in our hearts for these types of
over-achieving players. But Benny's talents go further. Benny,
like any great leader, can look through the lens of his fellow
man and see what is important to him and them. He is
unselfish. His leadership was a key component to our success.

Benny Holmstrom was not in this battle alone, far from it.
Nate Prosser was standing shoulder to shoulder with him in our
pursuit of excellence. Nate, in the past couple of years,. has
married and recently he and his wife had their first child, a
baby girl. In 2012 he signed his first NHL one-way contract
with the Minnesota Wild. A one-way contract means he makes

a big league salary whether with the big league team or sent to the minors. This is a big milestone for any player.

I didn't know this future was ahead of Nate on that night in Des Moines. What I did know was that we had a defenseman in Nate who could play in any situation, but most importantly, he cared. Nate wanted to win, period. He is a good Christian who values honesty and hard work. He epitomizes those values. Make no mistake, however, Nate can leave his nice-guy hat at the locker-room door and come to the *rumble rink* to rumble. Nate will compete and one will often see a mix of not-so-nice in his game!

In talking with Nate I told him the same thing I had told Benny, that I was writing this book and the only particular team I intended to talk about was his Stampede team that won the Anderson Cup-Regular Season Championship in '05-'06. To my pleasant surprise, he told me right up front the same thing Benny had said. *I want you to know*, Nate said, *that team is my favorite team I have ever played on. Like no other team, everyone was willing to leave their egos at the door and play for each other. We had so many great teammates, it was fun to be at the rink every day.* That wowed me again; he felt the same way Benny and I did. These are two guys who were captains at their respective colleges and are major league hockey players. Most importantly, we shared values. We shared values!

I asked Nate where he thought his great leadership skills had come from. *My parents, my faith, and my older brother,* he answered without hesitation. He continued on about his older brother and about how he was such a great role model for him: *I wanted to be like my older brother and I followed him everywhere*. Nate said that his brother wasn't a partier, that he wanted to do the right thing and over time Nate came to understand through his brother how to act like a man. Leaders role-model!

I have heard such a story so very often. Leadership is so often a 1:1 relationship. Role models role-model to one person at a time, even if many are watching. It's that one set of eyeballs that are on you that are always impressionable. Nate is a

Christian and most Christians will tell you that their faith is all about a 1:1 relationship with Jesus. There is a big lesson here and that is that we need to think about leadership first and foremost being a 1:1 interaction.

What really made an impression on me during this conversation with Nate was how much Nate appreciated this group of Stampede teammates. He went on to mention virtually the entire roster one by one, acknowledging the special talents each brought to the team. As much as he was one of their true leaders, his Stampede teammates and their unselfishness and commitment motivated Nate all the more. He could see through the eyes of his teammates how important this team was to each of them and this motivated Nate to serve each one of them by being a great role model and leader. Like Benny, Nate was able to get outside of himself and appreciate the experience through the eyes of others. Nate paid mindful attention to those around him and made choices in the best interests of his teammates.

We were having a great year that 2005-06 season; lots of wins and not very many losses, in a position to win the regular season championship. Upon leaving the rink after a game or practice, on numerous occasions I would call Benny and Nate over before departing, look at them both and remind them that we had something special going and that we needed them to take care of their team off the ice as well. Both would say, *don't worry about it coach, we'll make sure everyone keeps in line*. I never doubted for a second that between Benny and Nate, along with a number of our other leader-team members, that they would have control of our team off the ice as well. With 17-19-year-old boys, you always believe there is something to worry about, but with our leadership, I had confidence they would police themselves. This is always the best ally a coach has in keeping his boys on a good path; it is the players policing themselves.

These are the kind of groups-teams that really develop chemistry. Chemistry is so very hard to find at times. In the end, chemistry is developed when everyone shares values and buys into sharing their talents with those around them. And no one worries about who gets the credit!

Developing real chemistry is a challenge to most teams, whether they be sports teams or corporate teams. The higher you go, the more one will find successful people with more developed ideas of what right looks like, or how the organization should utilize their particular skills. At any level, it still gets down to values and unselfish service to team. This Stampede team of young men was on track and would continue to redefine itself and find the next new and best version of itself until the very end.

This team was going to win a franchise record 43 regular-season games. As the season progressed we all knew we had a good thing going. After home games, when I knew the girls would come a-chasing and if the girls didn't come, the boys would be tempted to do some chasing of their own, I would pull Nate and Benny aside and remind them what a good thing they had going and how rare it was to have such a great team. I reminded them to be good stewards and policemen and keep their teammates on the right path. They would both look me right in the eye and tell me: *No worries, coach, we understand. We'll take care of our team.* I never worried. I have never had a better twosome of captains-leaders. I am blessed to have been able to work with these two.

Then there is the story of another team member, Andreas Nodl. Andy has gone on to play a good number of games over several years in the NHL for both Philadelphia and Carolina. Andy took the ice representing his native Austria in the recent 2014 Sochi Olympics. Andy followed the path to Sioux Falls, a trail first blazed by fellow countryman Tomas Vanek. Vanek spent three years in Sioux Falls. Vanek was a scoring champion in the USHL and went on to the U of Minnesota where he helped the Golden Gophers to a National Championship before achieving stardom in the NHL. Andy was in search of a similar path to success in hockey.

In the Sioux Falls tryout camp that first year, I was watching this young Austrian Nodl who had already played a year in Sioux Falls with Nate and Benny and wondering what it was I wasn't seeing. Why wasn't I seeing a better player? He had very poor personal statistics from his first year and I wasn't hearing too many good things about him from those that had watched the team the previous year. People were talking about him like he should be cut from the team and sent back to Austria. About halfway thru the tryout camp that June, I called all the returning players into a room and let them know that it seemed apparent to me as a new observer that this group as a whole was not performing to expectation. I wasn't sure what I was seeing. Was it a sense of entitlement as returning players? How could they could feel any entitlement (as they had very little success the year before)? Whatever it was that I was and wasn't seeing, I let this group know they needed to earn their way each and every day and so on. Collectively, they needed to pick up their game and the time was now. To my delight for the remainder of camp, Nodl came to life. I had no idea what we had in him but at least I saw a sign of life.

In the exit meeting after the tryout camp I explained to Andy that even though he had a very poor first year with the team, I was willing to give him a chance, but no entitlement. Just because he had previously played on the team entitled him to nothing. He was going to have to take on the value of hard work and work his way up the depth chart. I told him that if he wanted to come back to our team in Sioux Falls he was going to start at the very bottom and would need to work his way up. If he could embrace that, he would be given every opportunity to make an impact with the team. I thought it was a harsh but honest conversation.

A week or so later, I got some very good news from his housing family parents in Sioux Falls, John and Joanna Anderson. They told me they had talked to Andy before he went home to Austria for the summer and they said Andy told them he had a great conversation with the new coach! Wow, I thought, I gave this guy a tough-love kind of talk and yet he was telling his host family it was a great conversation. This told me he might be ready to embrace the challenge. To make a long story short, Andy came back to Sioux Falls and was our leading scorer and the rest is history. In the end, he appreciated his success more because of the struggles of the previous year.

On top of it all, Andy was a humble, good young man who was also a good teammate.

Most of our key players had been humbled also. Mark Magnowski was our #1 center. He was traded to us, so he might have felt a little rejection from his previous team. I don't know that for sure. Mark was a smart kid and eventually went on to Princeton. Casey Parenteau filled out the Nodl-Magnowski line. Casey had already played in the USHL earlier in his career. Instead of playing for his White Bear Lake High School team in Minnesota, he left home his junior year for the Green Bay Gamblers. For whatever reason, the year did not go well. He returned to high school in White Bear Lake for his senior year looking, I suspect, like a failure to some. Subsequently he graduated high school, then went to D-III St. Johns for a year.

It could not have been an easy road to travel for Casey. In essence, he rejected his high school team for the USHL and then was rejected by the USHL and sent back home to his White Bear Lake high school program. That was a tough spot for a teenager and it appeared he had failed. Subsequently he gave up on his dream to play Division I hockey and went on to Division-III university St. Johns.

It just so happened that we also lived in White Bear Lake where Casey lived. I had gotten to know Casey. I got to coach him a bit as well in the High School Elite League. I thought he was an outstanding player. After his freshman year at St. Johns he heard that I had gotten the job in Sioux Falls. He called me and expressed confidence in me as a coach and thought if anyone could help him achieve his Division-I dream that was still alive, it was I. We talked at length about his possibly leaving St. Johns. He felt he had no downside to trying to make our team. If things didn't work out he could simply return to St. Johns.

Casey made our team and was a top player for us. He ended up the season as an assistant captain for us, leading our team along with Holmstom, Prosser and the other assistant captain, Magnowski. Casey ended up the Division I opportunity he had always dreamed of at St. Lawrence University in New York where he also became a captain. Casey was another young man who had been humbled and was hungry.

Our roster of humble lads didn't end there. Drew Aikens and Chris Berenguer, both Minnesota kids from good high school programs, had played in the Tier 2 NAHL the year before. Minnesota kids see themselves as the cream of the crop, so being relegated to the Tier 2 junior league is humbling. But Drew and Chris both put in their time in the NAHL and then made our Stampede team in their second year of Junior Hockey. Drew Aikens eventually became an assistant captain at U of MN-Duluth and Berenguer a captain and D-III player of the year at Hamline University in Minnesota.

Last but not least, was 5'6" Travis Vermuellen who also ended up a captain with Casey Parenteau at St. Lawrence University in New York. Travis will always be one of my favorite players of all time. He is a gifted athlete, but small for sure. His size was always an issue. I know when we picked our final roster I was asked at least several times by staff members if I was sure that I wanted to keep Vermuellen. It was no question in my mind; I was sure. And in this case, I was right. This kid's heart was bigger than his body, and his unique skill sets were amazing. He had this low center of gravity and cat-like agility. His soccer skills had developed athleticism in his feet. He was amazingly agile and the chemistry he had with Benny Holmstrom brought an element to our team that was irreplaceable.

Travis was another of our cast of characters to be humble and willing. Travis grew up being told he was too small for this and too small for that. He would need to prove them wrong often. He would again be told, *Well you got through this level, but you'll be too small for the next.* He proved them all wrong again.

Travis and Benny could match up against the other team's top players and be extremely effective. That night in Des Moines I would match them up with future NHL first-round draft picks Kyle Okposo and Trevor Lewis. Travis was our best defender against series MVP Okposo. The play I most remember from the game in Des Monies is Travis stealing the puck while we were shorthanded and scoring a huge shorthanded goal in a game we were going to win 2-1.

Defenseman Zach Redmond went on to become an NHL draft pick and an All-American at Ferris St. Zach made his NHL debut with the Winnipeg Jets. He has come a long way. Zach had a serious medial issue that summer that I will not go into for the sake of his privacy. But I will tell you that it was a dramatic illness that came seemingly out of nowhere. It was serious to where his parents rightfully became reluctant to allow their son to leave home for a hockey experience. Because Sioux Falls is a hospital community, the right doctors were in the right place to monitor Zach should any medical issues arise. Zach's year started out slow and personally frustrating for him. He was well behind his teammates on a variety of levels. He played catch-up on training and confidence. But catch up he did. I am so proud of this young man for all he overcame, it brings tears to my eyes.

It is not fair to name some and not all, but I could go on and on. Jake Drewiske went on to be a captain at St. Lawrence and first year player Corey Tropp went on to play in the NHL for Buffalo and Columbus after a great career at Michigan State. And there are many more. At the end of the day, it was the entire group, the room. Without question, it was the most humble and hungry group of kids I have ever been around. I wanted to win for them, and they for each other and us coaches. There was love and there was the chemistry it created.

That game on that night, and the great atmosphere in the Des Moines arena with a chance to force a final game for the USHL Championship back in Sioux Falls, will always stick with me because of the character of these young men and because of the true nature of their commitment to team. This was an elimination game and it meant everything to us. We were up against the wall in one of the great road atmospheres to be tested in. It was what you live for as an athlete. When you can go to battle with people you love and respect, well, you cannot ask for anything more. I have never been a part of a better group that I so wanted to fight alongside. That is the attraction of team sports and that night all the elements were there and we wanted and needed to win this game…and we did.

Winning this game forced a final and deciding game back in Sioux Falls. We lost that game five back at home 3-2. Their coach *Regg Simon* did a great job with his team. Kyle Okposo, a Minnesota kid who had also played at Shattuck, was named MVP of the series and he deserved it. He was amazing. He is still a star for the New York Islanders. Trevor Lewis, their other star forward, would also be drafted in the NHL's first round and would go on to win the Stanley Cup with the Los Angeles Kings.

As for our boys, I will not forget the stream of tears in the locker room after this game. They cared so much for each other. They gave so much and fell just a little short of that final goal. That said, I wouldn't trade that yearlong experience for anything. So many of these young men found themselves or redeemed themselves. But this team truly was humble. The team of players and coaches was truly committed to one another; a bond of love. There was no sense of entitlement. They played and slept and ate for their teammate next to them. They understood the value of *the room*. They worked with us coaches and helped us to do our job better. Along the way leadership was role-modeled daily. There existed a level of commitment that most "adult" organizations would be envious of.

John Wooden once said that competitors spend too much time trying to beat the other guy. He said in essence that the real battle is on the inside, trying to become the best one can be both individually and collectively as a team. I have always subscribed to that philosophy. The goal is to continually seek and find a better version of self. This Sioux Falls team could not have been more successful in that regard. A team picked to finish last, got every inch of talent and ability out of itself.

Throughout the years in Sioux Falls, I was always proud to hear our players in exit interviews talk about their time in Sioux Falls and be able to recite that they learned through their experience there that their mission was about a constant effort and focus on becoming the next best version of themselves as individuals as well as the team collectively. Our focus was always on our players and a mission for each of us to become another better version of ourselves.

CHAPTER 9:
NURTURING LEADERSHIP

The 2005-06 Stampede season was a success on many levels. My renewed interest in nurturing leadership was one of those successes. I had always believed in strong leadership but I had to admit to myself that while I may have played a role in the success of the team, the leaders we had on the team played the biggest role of all. And there was no question that in that regard I was more lucky than good. I was lucky to have such great young leaders in our room. All said, I was more determined than ever to nurture leadership in my future teams. We started on a mission to do just that.

In subsequent years, our organization had a great track record of nurturing leaders. It started with Prosser and Holmstrom and many others and the role-modeling they did for the next year's captains like Zach Redmond and Nick Dineen. All these boys ended up being collegiate captains. The next year's team was destined to win the Clark Cup championship with much of that foundation laid the year before by a group of committed players. We as an organization continued to value leadership and we set out to find better and better ways of nurturing it.

Our ownership shared in our mission. In the years to come, our main owner Bill Sexton would tell me on numerous occasions that he wanted me to know that winning is great and it is important but he was not so worried about that. *More than anything*, he told me, *I appreciate all all the captains are nurturing for the Collegiate Level.* He asked me to stay focused on that and *keep up the good work*! The fact that Bill took time to reinforce these common values meant a lot to me. It was strong reinforcement that we were moving the franchise in a direction appreciated by all stakeholders. We were a franchise with people in the important positions that were all "on the same page".

Fellow coaches Andy Jones, Kevin Ziegler and Zach Sikich as well as scouts John Rosso and Craig Sarner and I were all on the same page with the values we were trying to teach and reinforce. We scouted, looking for kids we thought wanted to be great teammates. We were on the lookout for players who would help us create positive chemistry in our room.

We took on the challenge of learning more about teaching leadership in an effort to be able to teach the concept better and faster. In the case of Junior Hockey, it is more like a trade school. You only get a player for one or two years, on a rare occasion for three. We began an active search for new ways of getting the players to understand more quickly that the concepts of leadership and great teamwork was an important step for us.

Andy Jones and I put this mission at the front of our thinking. We read what we could on these subjects, sharing the good articles and concepts as often as we came across something worth sharing. I spent one whole summer reading all I could about leadership concepts, which I did at our Rainy Lake cabin in the hockey-rich area of International Falls, Minnesota. At one point I read back-to-back books, one on the experience of a Navy Seal and one on the 450-plus-year history of the leadership of the Jesuit Priests. I realized quickly that the fundamentals of great leadership indeed are the same whether you are a Seal or a Jesuit Priest. But teaching these concepts was something we really wanted to refine and be able to accelerate.

This desire to find a way to accelerate the teachings of great teamwork and leadership was the genesis of our development of Challenge Weekend. One of our very first concepts was that we needed to break down pre-existing barriers, get all our team on some kind of common ground with common tasks and challenges, certainly away from the sport they all knew so well. We wanted our young players to face new challenges on equal footings. We wanted them to learn problem-solving skills and the leadership skills it took to solve the challenges, all away from the game of hockey and all the natural barriers that they shared.

Along the way in this pursuit, Kevin Ziegler did what he does best. With his outgoing personality and friendly nature, he ran across a new and incredible friend and resource in our Senior Chief Navy Seal Luis Nebel. Senior Chief, as we called him, was on homeland and part of a career day recruiting mission when our gregarious Kevin Ziegler spotted him. What started out with a *hey can you come talk to our team*, developed into a multi-year relationship where Senior Chief helped us design a more effective Challenge Weekend concept. It was much of what coach Jones and I envisioned, only better as he not only accelerated our learning curve on how to implement such a program, but made us better teachers and leaders.

GREAT LEADERS AND TEAMMATES MAKE EVERYONE AROUND THEM BETTER

Any drill or program that a coach, teacher or leader of an organization puts in place is only as good as its execution. As I heard many times from my parents when growing up, *the devil is in the details*, attention to detail is a key component in the success of any endeavor. Not only does the plan need to be good, but the details within the execution need to be executed properly. Senior Chief accelerated our knowledge and skill greatly on how to better execute the concept of Challenge Weekend.

With the help of Senior Chief our plan for Challenge Weekend evolved. Numerous team challenges, evolutions as Senior Chief called them, were designed that would be new experiences for each of our team members. Their successful completion would require superior teamwork, superior leadership with great communication and great attention to detail. We would put all players into leadership positions and learn through various team competitions. Seems simple enough!

We had 28 players show up each Labor Day to begin our preparation for the hockey season. After a month of pre-season training, we would keep about 23 players. We had a few more than we would keep, allowing for some pretty good competition for roster spots. Boys that were still in high school were guaranteed a spot on the team. Keep in mind, these high school boys had left home, left the comfort of their hometown high school and had already at that point enrolled in school in Sioux Falls. We could not morally uproot their lives and then not keep them on our team. Sending them home and disrupting their life and academics was not something we would consider. For all other players, it was time to compete for a roster spot.

For Challenge Weekend, usually the first full weekend we were together, we divided the 28 players up into four teams of seven. The very first year I recall putting what I thought were the seven youngest players on the same squad. These seven youngest were defined not just by age, but also by physical appearance and least amount of Junior Hockey experience. I put them all on the same seven-man team thinking that each might then be in a position to not be intimidated by a more experienced and more confident young man. I thought also this might allow a new leader(s) to emerge from this young group. It ended up being a good move. This young group ended up teaching us quite a few lessons and in the end won most of the challenges that first year.

Challenge Weekend was designed to be our three-day boot camp where all the fundamentals of what we wanted our team to be would be introduced and have some initial practice for all. The tone of the event was that indeed it would be challenging to both the individual and the team. We wanted them to know we wanted to find teammates who were willing to work together to meet a challenge. *We would be watching closely,* we told them. And we watched them closely. We were looking for winners, leaders, and those who wanted to be great teammates.

We had had them fill out a questionnaire coming into camp about what they thought leadership was and what qualities great teammates possess. We also had each of our boys read a book about leadership over the summer, so they had at least some idea of how to articulate what they thought leadership was. Then, of course, we had them do another survey after the weekend to be able to learn more about how their views on leadership and teamwork might have changed.

Our Challenge Weekend started on a Friday with a 2pm practice on the ice and went on thru Sunday evening. The boys would be tired when it was over. The 2pm Friday practice lasted until four and then the boys were given two hours to get some nutrition in themselves and be sure to bring back a full water bottle to where they were to report at 6pm. We started each challenge weekend at a domed athletic facility just a half-mile from our practice ice arena.

When the 28 boys reported back at 6pm, we had them assigned into one of four teams. Earlier in the week, each team had been instructed to make some team headbands or other team identification. Some made team flags and armbands. The boys seemed to always have fun with this.

Our team trainer was there throughout to be sure to care for any injuries that occurred prior to or during the challenge. Each of the four teams was assigned an observer/coach whose job was only to observe. The coach/observer's job was to pay attention to each and every detail in leadership and teamwork and the team's collective attention to detail so that accurate feedback could be given the team individually and collectively after an evolution. I have since conducted team challenges elsewhere and find that the role of the coach and observer is very important. The fact is that each team will have successes and failures. Accurate and honest feedback, as well as the facilitation of team dialogue, is essential for the team and its individuals to learn and grow from.

Challenge Weekend also proved valuable feedback for our staff. We were able to see early on who the great teammates and leaders were and this provided us valuable feedback as to what kind of kids we had on our team. We would only have some of these boys for a year so to get to know them at a deeper level early on, and that was important to how we might help each boy on a path of self-improvement. They evaluated each other as well. Their feedback also proved valuable in the identification of our leaders and boys we wanted to keep on the team.

Once the group organized at the 6pm report time, the games began. Senior Chief who I cannot thank enough as year after year, he took three days off to come and work with us, put the boys through some basic training. He started them off with a flurry of activity. After calling everyone to attention, he gave all teams instructions to select a team leader and report to him immediately...he gave them 60 seconds to do so. It was immediately interesting to watch how each team came to determine whom they wanted to send out as their initial leader. Many of these young men barely knew each other and certainly had not as yet had a substantive conversation with one another. A couple teams had more experienced players who knew or at least thought they knew who their leaders were, while some teams were truly starting from scratch.

Sixty seconds later there were four young men, each representing their team, standing in front of our Senior Chief excited and ready to get after helping their team to win the challenge put before them. They didn't know what was going to be thrown at them next. First it was explained and would be reinforced over and again throughout the weekend, that it was going to *pay to win*. Losing was not going to be an option and would come with consequences. The very first task for this new team leader was something close to the following; go back to his team and get each team member to sit in a specific way such as legs crossed with the left leg over the right, with the right hand on top of the left ankle and left hand on top of the right hand. There would be instructions for spacing. There would always be details to be adhered to.

He would let each team leader know that the first team to get it right would be rewarded. He would ask if there were any questions on any of the details and then implore them to not lose sight of *it pays to win* and certainly not to be the last to complete this simple task. Being last or getting it wrong was not going to be an option. After the captains exhausted the questions they had, they were told the competition was on! Quickly back to their teams the leaders would go and begin to organize and explain their team task. This simple little exercise set the tone for everything we were about to do.

Think about what this new leader and his team needed to do in a very short and what always ended up being a hurried period of time. The leader who had all the information necessary first needed to get all of his teammates' full attention. He would need to get them to understand that each of them was responsible to give proper attention to and execute all the details he was about to give. Some of these new leaders, a bit shy yet, did not in all cases have the self-confidence needed to get the attention of their troops. They also often didn't have an appreciation for how important each detail is. Of cuorse the other side of the equation were the teammates, many of whom hadn't yet in their young lives had a true appreciation for how to pay attention to all the details of a task. What seemed a simple exercise was executed incorrectly as often as it was correctly. There would be push-ups to be done!

Often with the help of the team observer/coach, the first lesson was one for the entire team. Each individual would be responsible to pay attention to each detail and then execute the instructions or the team could not be successful. Leaders need to know the details of the job and be able to articulate the mission clearly. Simple! Simple as it sounds, there would be plenty of mistakes in these many simple challenges. When a team got it right, they would be immune from the push-ups. If all the teams got it right, still one team would be doing push-ups for coming in last. You didn't want to come in last.

Details properly communicated and great execution came with rewards. Some teams began to get it right. Team leaders would be called back to Senior Chief and lessons of accountability would be shared. Losing was not an option...did this leader not understand this? Did they not understand the task? Were they able to communicate with their teammates and/or were there other breakdowns within the team? This leader would be given the same or at times a new task and continue until everyone got it right. The leader was held accountable for the actions and performance of his group. He had to learn to take charge and be demanding if necessary. But he learned that leadership comes with a lot of responsibility.

For teams whose individual members didn't really pay attention to the details, well, they learned in a hurry through peer pressure within the group that their lack of performance, of not paying attention and not getting the details right, was not going to be acceptable behavior. Winning had privileges and it was going to pay to win. Simple exercise and in many ways, the fundamentals of each game really didn't change.

The coach/observer played a key role for these new teammates. He could watch from a close distance and see why the team was performing well or not performing so well. After a few push-ups and a short break before a new challenge, the coach/observer could ask probing questions of the team so they could self-analyze what it was they were doing well and not so well.

Once teams were able to get through this first phase correctly, it was on to one of a number of other challenges that evening. The first major competition of a night which might be to walk a certain way with particular criteria as a team to a particular spot some distance away. There they might find some PVC pipes we had left behind with directions on how to get them filled with a particular amount of sand. Their leader would be instructed to seal them, once inspected, and then the team would proceed with a particular way to get the team back to our home base. Of course the teams that got all the steps right, and were first to return, won the event. Those unable to follow instructions, not completed in the allocated time or last place, found themselves doing more push-ups than they wanted.

As competitions moved along, we would have teams rotate in new team leaders so all team members would get multiple opportunities at leading their team. It took a lot of these youngsters out of their comfort zone. Teams that were successful had showed good leadership and interested team members that paid attention to details. The keys in team success for each task was:

*First, a good understanding of the task. Attention to detail.

*Learning to ask questions if they didn't fully understand the task.

*Learning to be sure to get everyone's attention and then to relay the task to the team and that included the forcefulness needed at the time to get their undivided attention.

*The ability to listen! The willingness to listen to teammates' questions and for suggestions from teammates on ideas on how to best attack the challenge.

*Then the team's collective ability to slow their minds and develop a cohesive idea on how to best attack the challenge. This includes constant feedback from team members on how to direct and redirect the effort. Leaders have to slow themselves down and be willing to listen when team members have ideas on what they think are better solutions to the challenge they are facing.

I mentioned the very young team we put together the first year of our Challenge Weekend. That young team won the vast majority of the events. They won the events for a number of fundamental reasons. First, they paid the most attention to the directions. No one seemed to think they were above anyone else, so they listened to all team members equally. Second, with their youthful enthusiasm and lack of pre-constructed barriers, they shared ideas freely with one another and came to consensus on how they best wanted to attack each obstacle. They were young, chatty (but focused) and enthusiastic!

For example, we had an underwater knot-tying competition at a local YWCA. All team leaders had to learn to tie four knots, each progressively harder than the one before. The team leader then had to go back to his team with a limited amount of time to teach each of his teammates each knot. Once the competition started, it was conducted like a relay race: each team member would go under water, tie the knot, come back and have the next team member do the same until all members got it right. Once inspected and deemed correct, they could move on to the next knot.

The young team, we had put together, had anticipated some difficulties, and were smart enough to develop some important strategies like having one team member become the *master* of each knot. Once put underwater to actually tie the knot, the pressure of the unnatural surrounding caused many players to fail. The young guys immediately put that particular struggling teammate together with their knot-master for that particular knot. It was a very smart move on their part. They won the knot-tying event by a large margin.

As the young team celebrated, knowing they had won the competition and there would be no pushups in their immediate future, Senior Chief went and stood directly in the middle of them and said nothing. Quickly they stopped celebrating and looked at Senior Chief and a team member asked Senior Chief, *What*? Senior Chief replied with a *what do you mean what*? Senior Chief continued: *You have three other teams still in the pool and most of them struggling, all of them your friends and teammates. What are you going to do next*? The boys were quick to say in unison: *Let's go help them*! But as they were about to quickly depart, one of these young boys called his team back and said: *Wait a second, get back here, let's figure out which team is struggling with which knot*. Good idea, of course. They did a quick survey and, of course, sent their team members most versed with the knot a particular team was struggling with to that particular team. Simple solution, yes, but it took someone to speak up with a possible solution/idea, it took the team to listen and put an action plan together. There was a reason the "young team" won most of the events. They simply were not intimidated by one another, freely offering and exchanging ideas with youthful enthusiasm and working together to find great solutions.

What this young team did may seem simple, but it is not. This young team and their great willingness to embrace being a team with many voices contributing to their success was not and is not the norm. Some of our more experienced boys and teams were either prideful, or stubborn or afraid to ask for help and appear something less than knowledgeable to their peers. These teams didn't fare near as well as our young team and the consequences were poor team performance and a lot of time doing push-ups!

Whether successful or not in each challenge, teams got valuable feedback post event from the coach/observer as to why they succeeded or failed. The young team's successes were no mistake. Watching them was a good reminder again for us coaches too. It is simple fundamentals that make or break teams.

Over time I got better at reinforcing these basic team values in all we did throughout the season. It is something all of us coaches need to remind ourselves. It is our job to train a good, functioning team…not just tell them how to perform a skill. For example, if we were doing a drill and one of the boys did it wrong, the first question I asked myself was: Did our team members have the necessary information to self-correct? If they did not, I needed to intervene and help this team member and probably the whole team with instruction and coaching.

On the other hand, if they had the information they needed to self-correct, it was then their issue of attention to detail and helping one another. I waited and watched to see if the team self-corrected. Often they did self-correct which simply required another player saying something like: *Hey Bobby, on this drill remember to…* But if they had the information and did not self-correct, that meaning Bobby went down the practice ice sheet and did the drill wrong again and no teammate stepped to his aid, I would blow the whistle to stop practice and yell out, *PUSH-UP POSITION!* Before we would start doing the push-ups I would yell out to the team: *Why are we doing push-ups?* Most often somebody would have the answer, yelling back for all to hear: *Because Bobby did the drill wrong again and we didn't correct him. That's right.* I would yell out: *Twenty-five pus-ups on so-and-so.* I would then expect someone to lead and for them to give us 25 push-ups in perfect unison.

What all this did, of course, was reinforce to the boys to be more self-reliant. If they didn't think they had the information they needed to perform a drill or an off-ice duty, they were expected to ask. They came to understand they were responsible for attention to detail. As I explained to the team many times over the course of Challenge Weekend and beyond, they were the ones out on the ice in the heat of the battle working together to get their task handled well. I was removed from the battle, far away on the bench and not in a position to help. Each of them needed to learn to lead, self-correct and know the details of the job at hand and then execute those details well.

With each day that passed, they got better and better at it. I could teach new concepts when needed, but they knew most often how to reinforce the old. They took charge of their own domain. The better I taught, the less I had to do because the boys took it upon themselves to hold each other accountable. Each team member knew it was important that they understood the details, as they would all be held accountable by each other. Each team member understood at a higher level than before they arrived how important each team member's efforts were to the collective effort. There was a real desire to help one another. It was a great process for sure and what I miss when I am not coaching: watching and nurturing a team coming together.

Over the course of Challenge Weekend, our stronger leaders rose to the top. Our weaker leaders demonstrated to us the areas they needed help with on becoming the leader we wanted each of them to be. We were better equipped as coaches to help each individual. Most importantly, our stronger leaders were better equipped to lead us on what is the very difficult journey of a season in the USHL.

When Challenge Weekend came to an end, we provided our players a questionnaire asking the boys to share with us what they learned about the fundamentals of leadership and becoming a great teammate. It was amazing all the lessons learned. Their knowledge of the true fundamentals of leadership and being a great teammate went from novice to much greater. And it was all fundamentals.

Also, we had the boys complete a peer review. In the peer review, each boy would rate each of his teammates on how good a teammate they were. The results of these peer reviews were most often not surprising. The boys recognized who their better teammates and leaders were. The peer reviews not only helped us identify the teammates that the team thought were the strongest teammates fundamentally, but those that needed the most help also. There is a saying that you might be able to fool the fans, but you can't fool your teammates. Even these young teammates quickly came to recognize those teammates that brought real value and ability to the team equation. As the season moved along, we conducted more peer reviews to monitor the progress of our young team members.

At times, if we felt it would be beneficial, we would share with a player that he scored low on the peer review. Any player worth having would not want to hear that he did not have the respect of his teammates and would ask why he scored lower. We would tell the player that we didn't do the rating, his teammates did. We would direct the young man to a team captain, maybe the captain this young man most trusted. We would instruct the young man to go ask this captain to be honest and share with him why he thought he was rated as low as he was. We would give the captain a heads-up so that they could prepare a good and honest answer for a teammate. Most often, the critical feedback from the teammate/captain had more impact than anything we coaches could have given the player. This process was impactful and put the development of the teammate at least somewhat back to where it is most impactful, at the team level.

It was a great process. These young men all had come from different backgrounds. They had different levels or preparedness for life. Some had great direction from family and friends, some not so good. We said over and over, at some point, every team member will assume a leadership role, be it on the ice or off. They had to be ready to lead when it was their time…no exceptions. Giving everyone a chance to learn about leadership and what it took to create a great team through the trial and error afforded these boys during Challenge Weekend (and the continual reinforcement) will remain the single best thing I have ever done for the teams I have coached.

NUMBERS DON'T LIE—OUR PROGRAM WAS WORKING

Somewhere along the mid-term of our involvement in Sioux Falls, our Director of Communications and all-around good guy Jim Olander came to me and said, *Coach, do you realize you have nine players serving as captains or assistant captains in D-I college hockey*? I did not, but I was really happy to hear that. I looked thru the D-I rosters, and that year could find no other teams in America with more than three. Our nine was a heck of a number. I thought that was about as good as it could get. I was pleasantly surprised to be wrong. The next year the number of our alumni serving in a captain's role at the major college/university level shot up to 15. No other team came close. Our alumni were being recognized in colleges and universities all over America by their teammates for having skills that mattered. They had leadership skills that teams of all kinds need. Leading teams is leading teams, be it big teams like a hockey team or small teams like marriages. These are real skills for real life. We were all very happy with the results. Oh, and we mostly continued to win.

CHAD RUHWEDEL—AN UNLIKELY COLLEGE CAPTAIN AND NHL PLAYER

In the 2012 college season, Chad Ruhwedel was named captain of the hockey team at the University of Massachusetts-Lowell and helped to lead them to the schools first NCAA Final Four appearance. Since then Chad has signed with and played with the Buffalo Sabres of the NHL.

On the surface, Chad may seem an unlikely candidate to be a captain at the major college level and an NHL player. Chad is a native of San Diego, California, hardly a hockey-playing hotbed. To make his ascent that much more unlikely, he did not do what most young aspiring players in non-traditional hockey areas do: leave his home at the start of his high school career. He remained in San Diego playing only AA hockey thru his junior year. He left for Los Angeles his senior year for his only year of AAA hockey. This is not a common track for a kid who would make a USHL team. Yet he did so in making our team after only one year of AAA hockey in Los Angeles.

We drafted Chad in the USHL entry draft. Chad made our team during tryouts showing great mobility and a better than average understanding of the game and an even better understanding of how to play his own game. He didn't say much in his first year with the Stampede but became a steady and very good player that first year for us. He was offered numerous Division I scholarships. He subsequently turned them down to play another year in the USHL. He felt that with his relative lack of experience, he needed to play at least one more year of Junior Hockey. It takes leadership and courage to turn down a sure college scholarship for the promise of only more development time. But that is what he did and in his case it was the right decision. In his second year, he became the team captain on a team that really came together and he was a big part of it. He became an excellent captain for us and also earned a scholarship at U-Mass Lowell.

Upon his exit interview, Coach Andy Jones asked Chad how it had come to be that a kid with a modest hockey upbringing from San Diego had become such a good USHL captain. Chad had an answer. He answered that there were two main reasons. One was our Challenge Weekend. He told us that when he was put into leadership positions during Challenge Weekend, he saw firsthand how his teammates would follow his lead and respect the direction he was taking them. This surprised him. It was obvious to our staff while watching Challenge Weekend that Chad had the respect of his teammates. Chad just needed to discover that fact for himself.

The second reason Chad shared with us was through a season long personal observation the year before. In Chad's first year in Sioux Falls where he said little, he had a great role model in then captain Dane Walters. Dane in 2011 went on to become an assistant captain for the Western Michigan University Broncos and then served as their captain and leading goal scorer for their 2012-13 team. Dane was one of our captains in Chad's first year. As Chad relayed to us in his exit interview: *Dane was one of the nicest and most popular guys on the team. But when Dane walked into the locker room, there was a different presence about him. Everything changed. He was ready to go to work and I just couldn't take my eyes off of him. I watched how he approached his work. I learned from Dane the focus it took to be successful and a great leader.* Leadership, at its most basic fundamental, is role-modeling positive behavior.

LEADING BY EXAMPLE

Each year, during our exit interviews, we would ask each of our departing players and in particular our departing captains for an assessment on who they thought were our returning leaders. They provided us great feedback. Then of course we went through Challenge Weekend again the following year which helped us further identify our strongest leaders that next year. After Challenge Weekend, we appointed our first set of captains for the year, sometimes only two, sometimes three. Then at each quarter of the season we rotated the captains based mostly on the feedback of our current captains and the information we got back from our players, own ratings via the peer reviews.

We would meet with our captains most weeks and ask them for feedback on how the team was doing, how the coaches were doing and what if anything they needed from us for the benefit of the team. We tried to encourage them to talk and us to listen. They were our greatest eyes and ears and really most times had a pulse for what the dynamics were within our team. They talked and we learned. They would come to us with problems both minor and sometimes more than minor. For example, they might tell us that they wanted cell-phone use restricted in certain areas like the locker room. They might make the argument that to restrict cell phones in the locker room would lead to mindful and focused teammates more aware of the team's dynamics. In such cases we coaches would just say, *good idea, get it done. Let us know if you need anything from us.* The captains made this happen. And maybe just as importantly, the team knew their voice mattered. They took ownership in *their* team.

CONTEMPLATION OFFERS SOLUTIONS

The success that the franchise had over our seven years had been nothing short of amazing. We won as many games as any team in the league. We advanced well over 90 percent of our players on to the NCAA Division-I ranks and have had as many players advance to the NHL as any in our league. But in the end, for me it was always an extra shot of gratification when I saw a former Stampede player be recognized for their leadership ability. The number of Sioux Falls alums who have developed into NCAA Division-I captains has been the most gratifying.

It has been an amazing run, influenced by the staff of Kevin Ziegler, Andy Jones and Senior Chief. There were other leaders along the way who indirectly influenced these boys, as well. I suspect our alums, our captains past, present and future, will be influencing many along the way in the future as well. In the end I hope that all of our boys understand their duty and obligation to lead in each facet of their lives, knowing they all need to lead. Better teams, better marriages, better relationships all around.

It is crazy how things happen, but Mr. Sexton sold the franchise. He had done a great job getting the Sioux Falls franchise up and running. He did so with great values and a caring for all involved at every level, and these great values that he lived permeated the entire organization. Like the Hubbard family, I could not have worked for a better man or better people. It was time for Mr. Sexton to move on and enjoy other parts of his life.

A new ownership group came in. In my initial meeting with the new group of owners, which lasted several hours, there is no doubt I felt they were good people, but there also was no doubt in my mind that they saw the world differently than I. I went home that night to my wife and shared with her that I would not be the least surprised if this new relationship did not work out. After all, there are lots of good people in this world that, when put together, do not make a good marriage.

In the end it didn't work out and it was time for me to move on. That said, in looking back, there was no franchise in Junior Hockey that, based upon wins and championships, players moving on to college, players becoming college captains and players advancing to the NHL, could claim more success. I was so lucky to have spent time on the same team as Bill Sexton, Gary Weckwerth, Kevin Ziegler, Andy Jones, Doug Schueller,

Jim Olander and Zach Sikich, along with great doctors, trainers, equipment managers and folks in the front office. And during this whole time, with the help of Zielger, Jones and Senior Chief, we refined a leadership program that was truly special. The results speak for themselves. We showed what could be accomplished with a common focus on a value we all thought was important. The collaborative effort and overall experience has helped me grow and I hope and believe that in life's next chapter, be it in coaching or elsewhere, to again be a better version of myself and hopefully make those around me that much better.

CHAPTER 10:
PARENTS MATTER

Wouldn't it be great if every parent were properly prepared before entering into parenthood? Wouldn't it great if both the mom and dad of a child had all the knowledge they needed, were home and committed to being the best parent they could be for that child? We all know children need role models and of course their most important role model is their parents.

Parenting is a tough job. Anyone who has gone through it knows how difficult it can be. Being a great role model for your children each and every day, being on your game so to speak, is a daunting task. Yet that is what we need to expect of ourselves as parents. The eyes of our children are always watching us. The observations children make while witnessing our behavior is critical.

I learned a lot during my childhood observing my parents. What I saw of my dad was a hard-working, no-nonsense guy. He came home at the end of a hard day, had a beer and sometimes two (extremely responsible with his adult beverages), got himself prepared for another hard day with a good meal, then read the evening newspaper, showered, shaved, and went off to bed to do it all again the next day. He didn't throw what little money the family had away on bad vices. He told us and everyone around us exactly what he thought. His honesty was never in question. He was a great role model. I was lucky to have such an excellent leader in my life showing me the way by being a great role model.

My mom was an old-fashioned mostly stay-at-home-mom. I don't know why this old-fashioned, selfless role of stay-at-home mom has lost its status in our society. My mom did all she did for everyone else but her. She made sure we kids got to doctors' appointments. She made sure that meals were ready for all and good lunches were packed for school. She made clothes for us and others. She lived for everyone else and arguably not enough for herself. Sounds like a pretty good parent and leader to me!

My parents did allow us lots of time to run about the neighborhood and be on our own—something many parents are afraid of today. In our current generation, we adults are much more directly involved in our children's lives. Our kids really have a lot of opportunities to watch how it is we behave and how they should be expected to behave when they become adults.

We parents travel with our children to their various activities, sometimes out of our respective towns for a weekend competition or event of some kind. Do we drive safely and responsibly? Do we treat the kids in the car properly yet with the kind of discipline kids need and deserve? Do we treat strangers with kindness and respect? Are we responsible with our adult beverages? We need to think about where, when, how…all the things we are going to expect our children to consider as they grow into adults.

Teaching and reinforcing the values we believe in are an important task in parenting. If we value and teach them *The Golden Rule*, we then need to role model it for them. It does little good to *talk the talk* but then not *walk the walk*.

We don't put the value of being a great parent high enough on our social pedestals. Society is great at placing high on pedestals athletes and entertainers whose God-given abilities might sell tickets to their various events. That said, their talents do not necessarily make them good role models. We should spend more time on the evening news highlighting great role models if we really want a greater society. What could be more important?

We have again entered a new social experiment as society does often, a new period of time where kids are in front of computer screens, video games and cell phones. In these media, moronic behavior in itself can make a "personality-celebrity" without any real substance or character. It is crazy. We have allowed our society to dumb itself down, and we are all to blame for that.

Personally, I cannot think of anything more important than simply sitting as a family, eating dinner together to talk about the day that each family member has had. Children need to learn how it is that people actually talk to one another. Lost for many are those days and long lost are the days where a couple of generations of family sat on front porches talking about the world for kids and grandkids to hear. Kids need parents. Unfortunately, in our society, too often it is kids having kids and they simply do not know how to lead or role-model. Too often, one or more parents are not there, maybe not even living in the home. It can be a difficult equation with the teachers being media screens from many sources.

Parenting is hard because it is time to lead most every day and most all the time. The eyes of our children are always on us. How we treat our spouse teaches our kids much about how to treat theirs in the future. We parents don't get a night off from that. But if the children see our love, the values that all we do are based upon, our concern for family and so on, they'll forgive our honest mistakes. We parents make plenty of them. But with values and love, our kids will in the end understand our imperfections while the values we live by will live on forever.

Parenting is such a complex job and there is no way to get it absolutely right. We each do the best we can with the talents we have. That said, we really need to work at this, especially in how we role model for our children. When we take them out to eat, we need to be sure to role-model great manners, great social graces in how we treat the wait staff...you know the drill. Many a good parent has suggested to their young adult as they are about to go out on a date to judge their date by how well or not so well they treat each seemingly unimportant person they encounter. Good advice, I think.

It seems pretty simple, but we each have to work at being a great parent role-model. I will share one story of when we got something right with our son Eric who at the time was an aspiring goaltender at Quinnipiac University. He went on to accomplish some pretty good things in his sport, but at the time he needed parent-leaders in his life. He did not need a shoulder to cry on or an enabling parent who would allow him to get off track through self-pity. My wife MaryBeth and I sometimes got it wrong, but in this case, I think we got it right. The following is a personal story of how parental leadership helped my son become USA Hockey's 2013 American-Born College Player of the Year:

Eric Hartzell is my son, well, really the son of my wife Marybeth. Eric is our middle child with an older brother Brandon and a younger sister Whitney. I say that Eric is really Marybeth's son because he looks like my wife's side of the family and he inherited many of his talents from his mom and his grandpa Jody Bidinger. Eric's mother was a state-scoring wiz in basketball, averaging 32 points a game her senior year of high school in Morton, Minnesota. This performance qualified MaryBeth as a Ms. Minnesota Basketball Finalist— one of five candidates deemed best female basketball player, in the state of Minnesota. She earned a scholarship to the University of Minnesota to play basketball. The day the University of Minnesota showed up to watch her play, it was against their best competition (Red Wood Falls), a team that would go on to win the State Championship. MaryBeth scored 51 points and the Golden Gopher coaching staff was there waiting at courtside to offer her an opportunity to play Big Ten Basketball at Minnesota.

As good as Marybeth is at shooting a basketball, she says she never beat her dad once. He was a freakishly good athlete. Well, our son Eric inherited all that freakish athletic ability. He has become an extremely hard worker in part because of the role models he has had in his life and also because he has firm goals he is trying to accomplish. On top of it all, Eric was blessed with size—six-feet four-inches of it. Today he weighs in at 216 pounds.

If anything was holding Eric back in his teenage years it was that he was a bit more immature than many of his age. For any young aspiring elite level hockey goaltender, I might argue that maturity is one of the very most important traits. I was lucky to coach Eric in Junior Hockey. As good as he was at times, he also had much room for improvement, especially on the emotional maturity side of things. I often said that the longer the development process takes for Eric and the more he matures, the more the great athlete will emerge. With Eric's strong goals and willingness to work to achieve those goals, time was his ally. Eric bought this time by playing midget hockey in Dallas. Then he played Junior Hockey for two years in the USHL in Sioux Falls before attending Quinnipiac University.

Quinnipiac University is a private college located in Hamden, Connecticut. Quinnipiac is known as a wonderful business and marketing school. The school has grown over the years and now hosts a great law school and most recently a medical school as well. Quinnipiac has one of the most beautiful campuses I have ever seen. It is not an inexpensive school to attend and his attending the school was made available to him only by the hockey scholarship he received. Hockey made his attending Quinnipiac possible. He was and is a fortunate young man.

Quinnipiac competes in a very fine college hockey conference, the ECAC. They play the Ivy League schools like Yale, Harvard and Dartmouth along with other schools founded many years ago, some before the Revolutionary War. This is a conference with great academic traditions and solid hockey programs.

Quinnipiac is a newer team to the conference. Quinnipiac became a major college, Division I competitor just within the past 15 years. They have the support of wonderful and appreciative alumni who built a beautiful hockey and basketball facility that could and does attract some of North America's top student-athletes. When Eric arrived his freshman year, the program had some previous small successes, but no ECAC championships and only one ever trip to the NCAA tournament. It was a young program waiting for a breakout year.

By any measure, Eric had an outstanding collegiate career. Eric finished his sophomore season at Quinnipiac as the fourth-rated goaltender in the NCAA in save percentage. In that sophomore season he also set a Quinnipiac single-season goals-against record, which he broke again in his junior season. In his senior season, he shattered all the records he had previously set. He became a Hobey Baker hat-trick (final three) finalist, a first-team All-American and was recognized by USA Hockey as American-Born College Player of the Year. His Quinnipiac team had an amazing stretch of 21 games without a loss. The Bobcats won their first ever ECAC title and advanced to the NCAA Final Four for the first time in program history. It was a team success fueled in part by a confident goaltender. There is no doubt Eric was part of an historic breakout year for the Quinnipiac Bobcats.

This story of parental leadership, however, is about Eric's freshmen season at Quinnipiac. After all his career success at Quinnipiac, it is easy to forget his freshman season. Even Eric might concede that it was his freshman year that changed everything…and for the better.

It was his freshman season that took some unexpected twists and challenged this young man emotionally. In Eric's own mind, he should have played more and maybe deserved better, but as is often said, through adversity comes an opportunity to achieve greatness. I love many of the great sayings about adversity, but bottom line, anything worth doing is going to be hard. The hard times are what make us. And for Eric, it was a harder freshman year than expected that may have "made" him.

This story is also about parenting and leadership. Eric's freshman year was full of calls home to his Dad, who is also a hockey coach. Being I was a hockey coach, possibly made my fatherly advice a little more credible to his ears but, in any event, I do believe that the leadership my wife and I provided as parents had a positive influence on Eric's positive mind-set and subsequent development.

Leading into that freshman year was Eric's last year of Junior Hockey in Sioux Falls as a 19-year-old, where he was being recruited by a number of college teams. The two that seemed most interested were North Dakota and Quinnipiac. I think any kid from the Midwest who is recruited by North Dakota is going to take seriously their advances, as their tradition and facilities are as good as any in America. After Eric's visit to Quinnipiac, however, he was nothing short of "smitten". Had North Dakota actually offered Eric a spot on their roster, I don't know if they would have changed his mind. In Quinnipiac, there were former Sioux Falls teammates who enjoyed the university and campus. The hockey facilities there in Hamden, CT., were simply outstanding. He could join his lifelong friend Zach Hansen also from White Bear Lake, and was told he could come in as a freshman and have a very good chance of starting. So Quinnipiac it was.

Being the every-game starter is always the first goal of a goaltender, though not easy to do as a freshman. Yet, it appeared Eric had a chance to accomplish such a feat. He started game one of the season at Ohio State. Starting the season's first game for your college team and as a freshman is an accomplishment in itself. At the time Ohio State was a Top Ten rated team and Quinnipiac went into Columbus and won. If I remember correctly, it was the first time the relatively young Quinnipiac program (as a D-I program) had won a road game against a top ten team in their school history. Great start!

The following weekend, Eric led off the weekend with a shutout—2-0 as a freshman starter! One could not ask for a better start to a college career. The twists of any career were already starting to turn. The following weekend, I receive a call from Eric on the Friday of a new hockey weekend and I could immediately hear the upper-respiratory "bug" he had contracted loud and clear. He was as sick as could be. It was time to get to bed and get better. He not only missed that weekend, but he missed the following weekend, as well.

Adversity comes in many shapes and sizes…Eric's came in the form of a harsh flu bug in addition to a teammate by the name of Dan Clarke. Dan Clarke was Quinnipiac's "other goaltender". Dan had a so-so freshman year, and I suspect the Quinnipiac coaches thought Eric would come in and take over the duties. Dan Clarke had different ideas. Clarke also won his first two games. When Eric went to the bedroom to recover, Dan Clarke led his Quinnipiac team to another four straight wins and Quinnipiac was off to their best start ever. When Eric returned three weeks later, he was sitting squarely on the bench watching Clarke play good hockey and helping his team win more games. Quinnipiac rose to a Top Ten NCAA rating for the first time in school history. Clarke was establishing himself as a reliable goaltender and Quinnipiac continued to win.

During this time, the phone calls home to dad began. *This sucks,* Eric would say, *I have done everything they have asked of me, I am 2-0 as a starter and I don't play.* I would tell him to *keep his mouth shut, be the hardest worker on the team and that his time was coming.*

Eric eventually played again and won—3-0 as a freshman starter. Then another start—4-0 as a freshman starter. In the very last game before the Christmas break, Eric started and lost for the first time as a starter in college. He was 4-1 as a freshman starter…a very nice beginning to a college career for sure. He should have entered Christmas break excited, as his first half for a freshman was pretty successful even though he anticipated he would play more. The next twist was on its way…to all of our surprise…after Christmas break, he didn't play a minute the remainder of the season.

Dan Clarke continued to be the everyday goalie and mostly played very well. The calls would come to me from a young man who did not want to understand. "You tell me my time is coming," Eric would say, "…but when?"

Even in my own mind, I found it odd that a young goaltender with such promise would be left on the bench so completely. Yet that is what was happening. MaryBeth and I were not on the phone calling the coach looking for answers or trying to give our son an emotional crutch of some kind. We simply stuck to the basics of love and leadership for our son. Our advice on the many phone calls we had never wavered. Never did either Marybeth or I say to Eric "you're getting a raw deal," nor did we feel sorry for him. Sure, as parents you hurt a little when your child hurts. But this was sports and just a part of life.

Life often teaches us our most important lessons through these adverse times. What we did say during this time was that it was for none of us to judge that he was being treated unfairly, but only that he had one mission and one mission only: a mission to be ready should he be called upon. His was a mission of improvement and preparation. It is all about when preparation meets opportunity and that day surely would come. I told him, often, that he had to outwork everyone on the team and to work with purpose as his time would come. Of course, one never knows when that time will be. I also told him that his teammates would see his efforts over time, as would his coaches. His teammates needed to be happy for him when his time came and willing to fight for him and with him. So that meant no complaining, being a good teammate and working hard and smart.

So Eric worked. He was the first one on the ice and the last one off. But to him, seemingly no one was noticing. I would reinforce the fact that the number one goal he has had throughout his life is to play in the National Hockey League, and that today's situation was just that—a situation for today. No matter his current situation, to someday be an NHL player meant there was much room for improvement, which meant much work to be done to be ready for that day. If that NHL opportunity was ever going to present itself, he had to be prepared.

At the end of what he would say was a disappointing freshman season, the coaches told Eric there was no harder worker on the team. In his mind, that was little consolation. Eric went to work that summer more determined than ever. Come the first weekend of his sophomore season, he didn't play again. In his call home, however, I heard a different attitude in his voice. It was a voice of quiet resolve. Quiet resolve in knowing he couldn't control certain things, he could only control what he could control. *This sucks*, is what I remember hearing him say, *but I can't control when I play, so I am going back to work*

Monday. In part what makes great goaltenders, or quarterbacks in football or athletes in general, is the ability to filter out the "stuff" that doesn't matter and remain focused only on what one can control. That said, at that moment in time, he wondered not just when, but also if he would play again. It was his quiet resolve that told me he had learned much from this situation and was more ready than ever for the challenge of becoming a reliable starting college goaltender.

As fate would have it, a trip back to Eric's home state was just the opportunity he was waiting for. Quinnipiac was scheduled to play St. Cloud State in Minnesota the second weekend of the year. Back in his home state, his coach felt it was time to show what Eric could do for the homefolks. Eric was told he would start in goal against the St. Cloud State Huskies. He knew he had to play well and likely felt as much pressure to perform as at any time in his life. The good news is he was prepared. Preparation was about to meet opportunity.

He had arguably prepared more and better than anyone. Quinnipiac won that game against a solid St. Cloud team. From there he played regularly, taking over the starting duties and went on to a 4th in the nation save percentage that sophomore season and began his ascent to elite stature as a hockey goaltender. That's a heck of a climb made only possible by a positive attitude, not polluted by a mind-set of victimization, but by determination.

Everything that happened from Eric's sophomore season on was amazing. His senior season was both the best for him individually and for that of his team. They all accomplished great things together.

Along with all the success, God has blessed Eric with size that is today's prototypical NHL goaltender. At season's end, he was courted by a handful of NHL teams as a free-agent, meaning he could choose which professional team to sign with. There were several great opportunities. Eric chose to sign with the Pittsburgh Penguins.

Time will tell whether Eric eventually plays in the NHL. He has given himself a chance in part by staying on track through the twists of his freshman year. He kept believing, working and preparing for that day. I believe we did our job as parents throughout his freshman adversity and reminded him of what was important. Eric had lots of growing up to do and I might argue he did his most important growing up when he went through that career adversity that freshman season. He is not only a better goaltender because of it, but also a smarter and better person who now better understands quiet resolve and how to stay focused on what matters.

He takes little for granted now. When the going gets tough, I believe he now more than ever before has the personal tools to better handle whatever life is going to throw at him. He will embrace the hard and he also knows that any adversity that comes his way is just a situation for that moment in time to be attacked with quiet resolve and a focus on what's really important. He has developed grit. With grit and the God-given abilities he has, he has a real chance to be successful at the highest level of his sport.

GRIT: THE REAL PREDICTER FOR SUCCESS

A note and reminder to all of us parents and coaches of young people: There is still no substitute for good old-fashioned hard work, especially when it is properly focused. In Eric's case we never delivered a message of how superb his talents were. Though we may have acknowledged his God-given talents, we most often reinforced the value of hard work and determination. I believe the next generation is going to need to truly *rediscover* the value of hard work. I say rediscover because I think at times our generation is sending our kids the message that using their brains and talents will get them where they want to go. Brains and talents are important, of course. Yet it seems to me that at times we are saying our hope for our younger generation is to avoid hard work, certainly the kind of hard physical work folks like my parents did back in the day.

The key is not to simply praise our young kids, tell them how wonderful and talented they are. That doesn't build self-esteem and it certainly doesn't build grit. Good old-fashioned elbow grease, getting out there and getting to work does wonders for self-esteem. In learning a work ethic, acquiring an "I can accomplish much by working hard and utilizing the talents I do have" is the way to acquire self-esteem and a can-do attitude.

True confidence almost always has an underlying value of hard work. Truly knowing what one can do comes with success achieved through challenge and a willingness to work hard to overcome more challenges.

As a final illustration: there was a study conducted of A-student achievers. They were separated into two groups. One group considered itself A-student achievers because they viewed themselves as exceptionally talented. I suspect they were often told so. The second group of A-student achievers believed they were achievers because they were hard workers. They likely acknowledged they had talents, but they viewed their achievement more because they were not afraid to outwork the competition.

In the study, the two groups were given a complex problem. It should be to no one's surprise that the "self-perceived hard workers" had a better rate of finding solutions than did the "self-perceived group with talent". I saw this same result often in my coaching as well. When given a difficult situation, most of us will revert to what we know best. In the case of the *talented* group, they would revert to their talents which already had not allowed them to find a solution. This often leads to frustration. Going back to the same special talent time and again when it doesn't work often ends in frustration. I saw this often with many of my talented hockey players. They had to be taught how to deal with frustration. The solution was showing them other strategies, other parts of their game that could be employed and that always included hard work and attention to other parts of their game.

On the other hand, the hard-worker group in the study also returned to what they knew best to solve the problem—hard work. By reverting to what they knew best, they simply kept after it, opening new doors, looking at the problem from different perspectives; doors opened only through perseverance. Maybe at times the wrong path was found; so it was back to hard work again. Through hard work and perseverance, another new door, a new thought, a new possible solution was explored. One can see why in the end the group of self-perceived hard workers had more successes.

We should acknowledge and reinforce our children's and students' special talents and abilities. But in the end, there is still no replacing perseverance and a good old-fashioned work ethic as a major value set. I have seen few athletes in my day as naturally talented as Eric Hartzell, but it was his hard work and perseverance that paid the most dividends in the end.

We parents need to reinforce our children's talents, but we cannot allow them to think talents alone will get them anywhere. False praise can lead them down this road to believing they can accomplish things without the needed amount of effort and sacrifice. There is nothing more valuable than a person with talent who is wanting and eager to work. Wanting to overcome adversity through putting forth an effort with the talents bestowed upon one's self…that is grit!

CHAPTER 11:
LEADERSHIP QUALITIES

To sum it all up, leadership is a number of things. We need to understand what it is so we can pursue it and recognize it when we see it. We need to understand it so we can encourage it in the people we love and especially in our youth. There is no time like the present to begin our nurturing of leaders everywhere. We will immediately begin to have better teams, big and small, which includes better marriages, better family units, better business teams and better sports teams.

First and foremost, everyone needs to accept the role of a leader. Every one of us has leadership roles each and every day. For a parent it is everything you do when your kids are watching you. Or in your marriage with just one *teammate*, what you say, what you forget to say, how you greet your spouse, and your body language, all matters. Likewise for those on a sports team or a corporate team with many teammates, it is each action and everything you do that is key. No matter your perceived role or importance on the team, each action and everything you do influences others in some way. Your tone of voice, your energy and attitude, all contribute to the chemical reactions that are going on around you.

The time to lead is not always a choice. Often it just comes at you when you're not expecting it and you need to be prepared. When your friend or family member has too many adult beverages to drive their car safely, it is time to lead. You may not have asked to be put in that position, but there you are. You do what you need to do.

Mostly, our roles as leader are much more subtle. It might be how we greet a stranger or how we respond to being slighted in the workplace. It can be how we respond to a friend in a time of need. Our actions can and will influence others. And when your leadership skills are needed, it has often been said that you can choose to be part of the solution or, by omission or poor leadership, remain part of the problem.

Leadership in its most basic form is leading by example. Leading by example is for that one person with their eyeballs on you at that moment in time. Those that consider themselves religious often refer to their faith as a 1:1 relationship with God. They follow the leadership principles of their particular faith. A parent setting an example for a son or a daughter is leading in a 1:1 relationship. There may be no more important leadership opportunity and responsibility as it lasts a life time.

In a sporting event, even if individuals do not see themselves as *the* leader, there will always be situations where they will need to lead. An individual basketball or hockey player verbally communicating on or off the court is leading others…one at a time. It is the helping hand, the kind ear or the tough love you help a teammate with. It is all leadership.

Even in big groups, it is the 1:1 message that matters. While many may be watching us at times, it is that one connection made by the observer that makes a difference. I cannot think of a more influential leader in my lifetime than Dr. Martin Luther King Jr. He led an entire movement throughout our great land. He may have spoken at any given time to many, but he still did what he did by influencing one person at a time. Individuals took his message with them and put their common values to work.

In the Chad Ruhwedel story in chapter 9, Dane Walters was in the locker room for all to see and while many may have been influenced, it was Chad Ruhwedel's mindfulness on Dane and his leadership skills which showed Chad the path to successful leadership.

Leaders define values for their mission. Most importantly, in the example of Dr. King, he lead by defining the **values** that he believed were important to him and to many others. He did it by sharing with us the *why*—why the values he believed were and are important. He explained why the mission was important in the first place. Dr. King got us to the emotional level of why; why we should put our heart and emotion into the effort. There is no more important motivation than that which comes from the heart...our emotional attachment to a project.

Dr. King did not become a great leader by telling people what to do. He left much of that up to us individually. He was a leader, an effective leader first and foremost because he shared with us his dream of higher values to the cause of civil rights. He shared with us the *why*, as to why a person who shares that dream might want to get off the couch and help facilitate change.

A leader will also follow, but will first ask the question: Is the mission, the *why*, worth pursuing in the first place! Many people from many walks of life did indeed share the values that Dr. King articulated so well. They shared that dream and decided to get off the couch and help or in many cases lead in their own way, to help realize the common dream they shared. Leadership is powerful stuff. Too often folks want to lead but make the mistake of telling their troops the what's and the how's. They skip the most important part which is the **WHY**. Leaders will follow the lead of others when they share the values that lead to a common motivation.

Love and respect are the basis of all leadership. Love and the heart are forever romantically linked. Love is the basis for any great relationship, from a marriage to a great locker room in sports. The first coach I recall using love as a concept was Hall of Fame football coach, Vince Lombardi. Coach Lombardi attended Fordham College—a Jesuit school where I suspect that the concept of love and understanding of fellow man were valued and reinforced. Love for your teammate seems pretty straightforward. If you love your teammate, you respect their growth as a human being and you want good things for them.

Love is not selfish; it is selfless. Love motivates one to be willing to help and even sacrifice for a teammate and team. Be it a marriage with just one teammate, or a hockey or corporate team with 20 teammates, if what you do is to use your talents for the betterment of your team and teammates, others will respect your efforts. Love and respect of your teammates, respect of their desire to be the best version of themselves is a powerful motivation. When teammates know you want the best for them, when your actions are true to this cause, your ability to lead them will know no boundaries.

In the case of Dr. King, the values he shared had to do with love for his fellow human beings. Many others shared his values. When you respect the project you are working on, respect the effort, then you can truly put your heart and soul into the effort and accomplish great things.

Leaders need to listen to gain the knowledge they need. This is an underrated element of leadership. We all know we learn more from listening than we do from talking. Leaders seek good information. Leaders are always trying to learn. Leaders in industry hire people smarter than themselves in many areas for the benefit of the team and its direction. Leaders need to collect good information from those around them.

Leaders need to be mindful. Wherever the thought or idea comes from, a leader will give proper thought to the idea. Leaders do not just find new directions or paths mindlessly. No one will follow a fool, at least not for long! Leaders need knowledge and they obtain this knowledge by seeking information.

In the pursuit of knowledge, leaders also need to take time to get intimate with their own thoughts. Leaders need to know what they believe. Dr. King was involved in many civil rights issues and knew where he stood on them. The development of his thoughts and values did not happen overnight. This great leader took years to develop his ideals and values. He was solid as a rock...he knew what he believed and that is why this great leader could so perfectly articulate the issues he felt so profound about to so many.

Many times the first idea or thought one is exposed to, be it their own or something heard from someone else, is no more than a stimulation of sorts. While this new thought or idea might be interesting, it most often will go through its own metamorphosis developing into something more concrete. Getting intimate with your own thoughts, allowing them mindful time to grow is very important and sometimes hard in our current world of constant movement and information flow. Great leaders use time to allow for contemplation of their thoughts as well as actions current and future. In the end, like Dr. King, one must believe in their mission, must believe in their WHY if they are ever going to influence others.

Solid beliefs and values lead to good and confident decisions. When one acquires great knowledge and allows it time to evolve within, then and only then will one be able to make a good decision under duress. Without a developed understanding of how and what one really believes, under duress chances of a good decision are being left more to luck. You have got to KNOW what you believe.

   Leaders demonstrate confidence. Confidence is a funny thing. It grows from mindfulness, patience, practice and doing a lot of things right until you KNOW you can do it or believe in it. Leaders portray confidence because they have done their homework. They believe in their values. They have allowed their thoughts time to develop.

   Because leaders believe in their values and have the knowledge needed to make decisions, they set out on paths with clarity and confidence. After all, leading can mean taking a path others have not. This new path may be great and it may also have its own challenges not before seen. But leaders, once understanding their mission, will see new paths, often times influenced by others with a similar vision, but always with an understanding of WHY the path may be worth the risks and effort.

Leaders are not always right. Leading is tough. It is not always going to be the case that a leader looks back and says that the right choice, the right path was taken. There are lots of paths and lots of paths off of those paths. There is risk-taking in leading. Even if the best path is chosen, not everyone is going to see it that way. Leaders have confidence that their choices are good because of the mindfulness they give to the values and the various factors in their decisions.

To be a leader, to lead a group down an alternative path, means of course there may be new and unforeseen benefits. It also means that, at times, one will choose a new path that is not as good as hoped. Some call this being wrong. Being wrong is generally thought of in our society as a negative thing! If we could all buy into the idea of being wrong as part of a larger process in the discovery of finding better ways, we all would be better off. Players and teammates have to be allowed to make mistakes to expand their games and positions. Leaders have to be able to do the same with their own evolution. Finding the truth, searching for a better course often is littered with mistakes; the wrong direction, the wrong assumptions, the wrong tools or just plain wrong thinking. The only way we discover that we were wrong is a constant search for better. In a lot of cases there is no right, just better or best for the moment.

Coaches who coach the first game of the year the same as the last game of the year are likely never going to achieve greatness for themselves or their team members. The same goes for parents. As we all know, we all need to make some of our own mistakes along the journey. Teammates, kids and workmates all need to have some room for error and expanding their own skill sets and knowledge. It takes courage and confidence to give individuals this freedom, but it can be done with some level of guidance and direction based in love.

Leaders need to be open to new ideas. When a leader accepts input from others, with sincere appreciation for a teammate's willingness to share their thoughts, it nurtures an atmosphere where more team members will offer thoughts and take more chances. New ideas may replace old. Old assumptions may prove to be wrong-minded or maybe just a little off target. In any case, being wrong at times is just part of the process. Being unafraid to be wrong is right.

New ideas, new directions and being wrong has its limits. One would never want to risk the lives or safety of his or her team. A corporate leader would not want to take a chance with a direction that could permanently harm the corporation without mindful consideration. All of us who have parented teens know that it is a tricky balancing act between allowing freedom for our children to choose directions and the boundaries they need to keep them safe from many factors surrounding their lives. That's risk management and there has to be some common sense to that, of course. But when all is said and done, making mistakes is part of the process of finding greatness.

IN SUMMARY, LEADERSHIP IS...

• THE ABILITY TO BE ABLE TO THINK FOR ONESELF

• THE ABILITY TO ACT ON ONE'S OWN MORAL CONVICTIONS

• THE ABILITY TO USE ONE'S KNOWELDGE TO BE ABLE TO DIRECT AND/OR REDIRECT AN EFFORT

HOW DOES ONE GET THE SKILLS AND KNOWLEDGE NECESSARY TO LEAD?

• SEEK KNOWLEDGE. LEADERS ARE MINDFULL OF ALL AROUND THEM!

• LEADERS DEVELOP THEIR KNOWELDGE; THEY GET INTIMATE WITH THEIR OWN THOUGHTS. FIND TIME TO CONCENTRATE AND FOCUS TO FURTHER DEVELOP YOUR OWN THOUGHTS.

IN THE END, WHAT DO LEADERS DO?

• THEY DON'T JUST ANSWER QUESTIONS, THEY ASK QUESTIONS!

• THEY DON'T JUST FULFILL GOALS AND TASKS; THEY SET GOALS!

• THEY DON'T JUST GET THINGS DONE; THEY ASK WHY THE PROJECT IS WORTH DOING IN THE FIRST PLACE!

• THEY FOLLOW PATHS AND THE VALUES ARTICULATED BY OTHERS OF WHICH THEY BELIEVE IN YET USE THEIR KNOWLEDGE AND CONVICTIONS TO DIRECT AND REDIRECT THE EFFORT.

• THEY DON'T JUST SHARE THEIR VISION OF THE PATH THEY HAVE CHOSEN, THEY SHARE WITH

OTHERS <u>WHY</u> THEY HAVE CHOSEN THE PATH THEY
HAVE CHOSEN.

CHAPTER 12:
GREAT TEAMMATES; GREAT TEAMS-GREAT LIFE

Be it a small team like marriage or a large corporate or sports team, we all should strive to be great teammates. Being a great teammate, having great teammates, for me it is what makes the world go-round. Who doesn't want to be or have a great spouse? Who would not prefer to have a great bunch of teammates at work? Being a great teammate requires some skill but mostly lots of "want to". Great teammates who have great leadership skills can achieve much.

The following is a guide for the fundamentals it takes to be a great teammate:

BE YOUR OWN BEST COACH AND LEADER:

Athletics and life are best approached with sound fundamentals. Most of these fundamental "things" you can control. Can you self-direct your own progress? Can you lead yourself? Are you part of the solution or part of the problem? Do you seek solutions to a poor relationship, be it with a teacher, a spouse, a coach, a teammate or a friend? Commit yourself to being part of the solution.

GIVING:

Are you able to look outside yourself and see how others see things? Do you think of your talents as something you want to share? Maybe the biggest fundamental of the Christian faith is *giving*, which is why we *give* at Christmas. There is an old saying that "it is more blessed to give than to receive." This is the simple belief and I believe to be a truism—the more you give, the more blessings you get in return.

Do you use your gifts to make those around you better? Do you make your team better? your boyfriend, girlfriend, husband or wife better? The best relationships are the ones where each member makes the other member(s) better. To evaluate any relationship, simply look at each member and ask what each does to make each of the other member(s) better.

DUTY, OBLIGATION, SACRIFICE:

How is it that a soldier can throw himself or herself into a line of enemy fire on the battle field, or how can firemen run into the Twin Towers on 9/11 knowing full well the risk? DOING WHAT IS NEEDED/REQUIRED WHEN IT IS NEEDED/REQUIRED IS DUTY AND OBLIGATION! Being in a marriage or on a sports team, in the military, the fire department or any corporate team, all have fundamental duties and obligations. Be accountable, reliable, and dependable for the sake of your teammates and your team!

POSITIVE ENERGY and ATTITUDE:

We all know we are in control of our own attitude. Attitude and positive energy are so important. And what's really awesome about it is...IT IS CONTAGIOUS! Unfortunately, so is negative energy contagious. Most successful organizations will not compromise on the sporting of a positive attitude. If you aspire to a better marriage, a better corporate team or sports team, bring your positive energy every day.

STEWARDSHIP:

Take care of those things entrusted to you. Help build and/or improve the program or organization you are a part of. Contribute as best you can to its long-term health and well-being. Being a good steward extends past your marriage and your team, it is the university you attend, the golf course you play and the earth we live on. If you can use your talents to make each and everything you come in contact with better, you will have made a great and positive impact.

HONESTY:

One of the big reasons people fail as individuals and within relationships…lack of honesty. One must honestly assess their situation. One needs to honestly consider their strengths, their problems, and their challenges if they ever are going to find an effective path forward. Look in the mirror, self-assess with an open and honest mind. With proper mindfulness one can find an effective solution. Learn the art of meditation for self-reflection. The same goes for a team and its challenges—they must first positively assess the challenge, then make a plan, make adjustments when necessary and then execute. The Senior Chief Navy Seal we worked with in Sioux Falls had a saying: identify, adjust, and execute. But it must all start with honest identification and assessment.

Seek honest feedback from those around you. Seek this honest feedback from those who care about you personally like your parents and mentors. Seek honest feedback from those with expertise in the sport or field of pursuit, like your coaches and other mentors within the field, then take all that honest feedback, and deal with it honestly.

JEALOUSY:

Jealousy is an individual's landmine. Jealousy is worry about what others get. Are **others** getting more love, attention or praise as compared to ME? Jealousy can cause irreparable damage to the individual's own soul and to the relationships in their life. Jealousy can quickly tear down a team with worry about what others are getting instead of staying focused on giving and focused hard work for the benefit of others. Embrace and appreciate the success of others! Embrace the acknowledgment others receive! Not doing so just allows negativity within.

We are not to judge the successes of others, be theirs born of good fortune or earned. More likely their success came through hard work, often not witnessed by us. In any case judging the effort and good fortune of others is futile and does nothing to help our own situation. Focus on your own mission and how to serve others around you. In the end, you'll be a lot happier.

ATTENTION TO DETAIL:

Do you know exactly what is expected of you? If you don't, do you ask? Do you know what is expected of each of your teammates and how it integrates with your job? Great teammates make it their job to know and understand the details expected of them (and others) to do a great job for the benefit of the team and their teammates.

LEADERSHIP-PRINCIPLED AND POSITIVE VIEWS TO DIRECT AND REDIRECT THE EFFORT:

Do you care enough about your team, your relationship(s) to share your principled knowledge to better the team-relationship? Do you pay mindful attention to the dynamics of your team, allowing thoughts and ideas time to develop? Do you then lead with your knowledge? Lots of efforts fail because the person with the best solution doesn't speak up. Be a *leader* and be true to your values; express your ideas for a new and better course when needed. Likewise, listen to and value the ideas of other team members!

CLIMB THE MOUNTAIN:

Be committed to the pursuit of excellence. Our world changes quickly and without commitment to constant improvement, you will be rendered obsolete. Ask yourself, if you were in need of a potential life-saving operation, would you want a surgeon who was still using technology and knowledge from just 10 years ago or would you prefer a top professional who has up-to-date technology and knowledge? Choose to be a TOP professional and commit to constant improvement.

Perseverance is often the key. The solution to today's problem or the desire to improve one's position may not be apparent today. There is no replacing good old-fashioned hard work in pursuit of finding new ideas, new solutions and places never before discovered. Little of consequence ever comes without hard work in the direction of achieving a goal.

THE GOLDEN RULE:

Do unto others, as you would have them do unto you!!!

Kevin Hartzell grew up in St. Paul Minnesota. Kevin grew up the son of an Iron Worker Eugene, who also served as the president of Iron Workers Union-Local #512. Kevin was a multiple sport athlete who rose to be a captain on all of his various sports teams including the St. Paul Vulcans and the prestigious University of Minnesota Hockey Team. Kevin was a member of a National Championship team at the University of Minnesota under legendary American hockey coach Herb Brooks. Kevin also guided the St. Paul Vulcans and Sioux Falls Stampede teams to National Championship games five times, winning the National Championship two times.

Leadership development has been one of Kevin's passions. In 2005 in Sioux Falls, Kevin implemented a leadership program with his Sioux Falls USHL team. The leadership program produced unprecedented results as measured by the number of captains produced for the NCAA Division I universities.

In his early years, Kevin was fortunate to work under the guidance of Hubbard Broadcasting both as a National Championship hockey coach and eventually on the Television Sales team where he rose to a leadership position as National Sales Manager. This all happened at the time the Hubbard family was pioneering what we today know as DirectTV.

Kevin has been a writer for the Midwest's leading hockey publication, Let's Play Hockey, since the late 1980's. Kevin has been married to his wife Marybeth for 29 years. They have three children.

To order Paperback or ebooks please go to Amazon.com

To order audio books: Audible.com or Amazon.com

To contact Kevin Hartzell and Leadership Enterprise Group (LEGgroup), please send email inquiries to **LEGgroup@outlook.com**